Praise for *Don't Go*

"*Don't Go* is a remarkable piece of work that can change how we all live. The human voices and engaging, innovative approach do more than a mountain of data ever could to bridge racial barriers. This is a powerful and compelling book."

Lawrence D. Bobo, Harvard University

"The first-person accounts in this book are a powerful reminder that segregation isn't just about points on a map; it's about the geography of feelings inside those growing up within its shadows. *Don't Go* lays this bare, while also giving space for hope that change will come – and how."

Henry Louis Gates, Jr., Harvard University

"This book provides a challenging but beautiful reflection on the reality that many Chicagoans know to be true but too often don't know how to talk about or address. In sharing real-life personal accounts, the book invites everyone to consider the power of stories and relationships as a weapon of separation or a tool for healing."

Candace Moore, Senior Strategic Advisor at Race Forward
and Inaugural Chief Equity Officer for the City of Chicago

"Every one of us, no matter how much we're committed to racial justice and believe in racial equality, has stereotypes that we need to overcome. If you think you're immune from the stereotypes of 'dangerous Black neighborhoods,' you should read this book."

Richard Rothstein, author of *The Color of Law*

"*Don't Go* is the much-needed, cross-disciplinary, collaborative tome on how segregation and fear keep cities like Chicago divided. Tonika Lewis Johnson and Maria Krysan frame the complex subject of racism and geography as both a deeply personal narrative and a profoundly systemic problem. As has become Johnson's signature style, in *Don't Go* she has masterfully blended the poetics of Black life with the very real human emotions – such as uncertainty and misinformation – that keep us all from feeling more connected."

Amanda Williams, Chicago-based artist and 2022 MacArthur Fellow

DON'T GO

DON'T GO

Stories of Segregation and
How to Disrupt It

TONIKA LEWIS JOHNSON
AND MARIA KRYSAN

polity

First published in 2025 by Polity Press

Polity Press
65 Bridge Street
Cambridge CB2 1UR, UK

Polity Press
111 River Street
Hoboken, NJ 07030, USA

ISBN-13: 978-1-5095-6444-6

A catalogue record for this book is available from the British Library.

Library of Congress Control Number: 2024933713

Typeset in 11 on 15pt Dante MT
by Cheshire Typesetting Ltd, Cuddington, Cheshire
Printed in Canada by Marquis Book Printing

For further information on Polity, visit our website:
politybooks.com

CONTENTS

KEY NEIGHBORHOODS
MENTIONED IN THIS BOOK

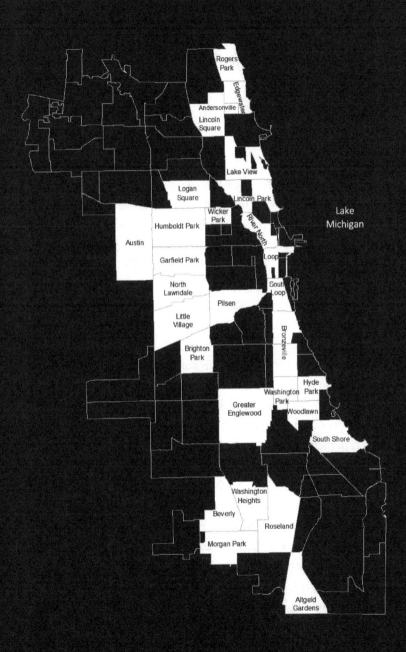

FOREWORD
BY MARY SCHMICH

I was scrolling through Facebook one day, musing on what to write about in my next *Chicago Tribune* column, when I landed unexpectedly on the perfect topic. There in the stream of pet photos, birthday greetings, and vacation selfies was a short video that showed Tonika Lewis Johnson talking to freshmen at Northwestern University.

"By a show of hands," she asked the group, "how many of you all are not from Chicago?"

Most of the hands went up.

"By a show of hands, how many of you all have been told to not go to the South Side or that it's dangerous?"

Again, almost every hand was raised.

"So," she told the group, "there lies one aspect of how segregation is perpetuated."

At the time, in 2019, I'd never met Tonika. I'd heard of her Folded Map project, in which she photographed homes at corresponding addresses on Chicago's North and South Sides. The photos showed how racially segregated the city is, how unfairly the city's resources are distributed.

Of course, segregation and inequity are hardly new. They're the enduring cracks in our shared Chicago life. But Tonika has a knack for finding novel approaches to these tenacious problems, and in her Folded Map explorations, she went beyond taking pictures and naming the issues. She met the people whose homes she photographed. She introduced them to each other. She got the North Siders talking to the South Siders. She got them thinking.

That's Tonika's brilliance. She gets people talking. Thinking. Looking for solutions. She did it with Folded Map and she's doing it again with the *Don't Go* project.

The day I stumbled on her "Don't Go" Facebook post, I instantly recalled my arrival in Chicago to write for the *Chicago Tribune*. It was 1985. I'd spent my life in Georgia, Arizona, California, Florida, and France, and I felt like a foreigner in this vast, northern metropolis. I knew little about the city's racial history or geography.

But I soon learned – meaning I was told – that there were streets I shouldn't cross, neighborhoods I shouldn't enter. Some of those places were on the predominantly White North Side, where I lived, but most were on the South and West Sides, home to most of the city's Black residents. In fact, it soon became clear that the terms "South Side" and "West Side" were common shorthand for "poverty" and "danger," never mind that such reductive thinking overlooked the deep, rich life that also existed in those parts of town.

A few months into my new job, I heard about a woman who was running a theater program for residents of her West Side neighborhood of Lawndale. When I proposed a story on her and her program, an older colleague, a longtime Chicagoan, shook his head. It's dangerous, he said, don't go there.

I went anyway.

The cab driver I hailed outside Tribune Tower downtown grumbled when I gave him the address, but he took me, warning that I'd have to call for a taxi home since cabs were hard to find in Lawndale. When the interview was over, I called. I waited for the cab for two hours. Getting a ride home, as it turned out, was the only trouble I encountered.

In the following years, I heard many more "don't go" warnings. Some, frankly, were reasonable. Others, though, were rooted in poorly informed stereotypes, which was what resonated for me the day I saw Tonika's Facebook post.

So I tracked her down. We talked. And I wrote a column about her "Don't Go" presentations. Responses poured in.

Some people wrote to say thanks, or to report their positive experiences in neighborhoods unfairly painted with the broad brush of "dangerous." Others warned about the "naivete" of suggesting people travel across the "don't go" boundaries. Some said they'd like to visit the South or West Sides but didn't know where to start. Or they worried they'd been seen as woke tourists, voyeurs, intruders. A few responses were flat-out racist. All of them, together, illuminated how complicated it is to change neighborhoods and minds. This book is an attempt to help make that change.

In these pages, Tonika and her collaborator, sociologist Maria Krysan, interview 25 people* who reflect on their own experiences of being told not to go to the South or West Sides. No two stories are the same. Every single one is moving, and thought-provoking. So are Tonika's and Maria's reflections – included with the interviews – on the stories they've collected.

I was lucky in my years as a *Chicago Tribune* writer to have work-related reasons that made it easy for me to disregard the "don't go" warnings. My reporter's notebook was my calling card, and it allowed me to meet people I probably otherwise wouldn't have, to sit and converse in their living rooms and kitchens and churches. Those encounters taught me to see Chicago more fully, and love it more deeply, a process that never ends.

---

* Observant readers may wonder why we say 25 interviews when there are only 24 individual stories mentioned on the contents page. This is because Emily's story is included within the "Sociologist's Notebook" chapter.

This book will help many people see Chicago more fully. And while solving the "don't go" problem isn't as simple as telling people, "Go," Tonika's and Maria's work helps us confront the myths and mindsets that make it harder for Chicago's very real problems to be solved.

Don't Go sends a message: Let yourself listen. Let yourself learn. Let yourself think about how you learned what you think you know. And then go somewhere that broadens your view of your city, your fellow citizens and, maybe, yourself.

ACKNOWLEDGMENTS

Don't Go was viewed by some as too much of a downer title for what is our book's inherently optimistic message. And so we express our gratitude with a similar juxtaposition: negatively disguised positivity.

No *project* without our storytellers.

Twenty-five complete strangers were willing to go along with us on this ride. Destination unknown. And we said as much when we started each zoom call with the person who emailed "foldedmapthoughts@...." with their stories. None of it would have been possible but for the kindness, generosity, humor, and commitment of the Chicagoans (lifelong and transplants alike) who shared their stories. To you all: We appreciate and respect each one of you for letting us tell your story, so that others may be as inspired, informed, and impacted as we were.

No *financial wherewithal* without UIC and CCT.

The University of Illinois Chicago gave us a Creative Activity Award grant and the flexibility to pivot and morph the project during a global pandemic, and the Chicago Community

Trust's longstanding support of Tonika and the Folded Map Project kept us moving forward.

No *test run* without *Block Club Chicago*.

Editors Dawn Rhodes and Jen Sabella helped us turn our raw interviews into newspaper-style stories, published them, and hosted a public event. The response assured us that these stories needed to be shared.

No *stories* without Mary Gustafson.

Mary was our loudest and most reliable cheerleader during the long process from interview data to sociological reflections to engaging stories. She helped transform academic writing into creative (read: accessible) writing, and penned beautiful Tonika, Maria, and Tonika + Maria stories.

No *book* without Jonathan Skerrett.

It was a long and circuitous route that brought us to pitch – in keeping with the project, over a zoom call – this "Academic + Artist" book project to Jonathan at Polity Press. And he "got it" immediately. And embraced it. He has wowed both the artist and the academic (that has to be hard, right?) with his skill, enthusiasm, and vision; and his ability to encourage, nudge, and shed light on the process. Every step of the way.

No *supporting materials, expert advice, and early readers/reactors* without Team Don't Go.

The roster includes Mary Schmich, Joshua Tootoo, Sarah Rothschild, Janell Nelson, and Michelle Harris.

No *foundation* without our families.

Our photographer dads (Tony Lewis, Jim Krysan), artistic moms (Rita Lewis, Carole Krysan), and our respective put-us-in-our-place and who-we-do-it-all-for children – Nyjah, Khayyel, and Katerina.

No *fun* without our friendship.
A friendship born out of disrupting segregation.

WHAT THIS BOOK
IS ABOUT

It doesn't take a trained psychologist to diagnose the root cause of the "Don't Go" warning. Fear. So yes, this is a book about fear. It also doesn't take a trained sociologist to tell us that fear is complicated. But what happens when it's an artist who poses the question? An artist who is from a place people are told not to go? An artist who is all about making segregation personal and about taking a simple question and unpacking it to reveal the humanity and the larger story?

This book is what happens when that artist teams up with a social psychologist to talk to "regular people" about what is a seemingly mundane bit of advice dispensed with great regularity. Not just in Chicago and its South Side, but in cities all over the country where there is segregation (and there's a lot of places like that). Don't Go.

This book is about fear . . .

Fear of being hurt (like shot or killed, it turns out),

Fear of being embarrassed,

Fear of being uncomfortable.

It's about how this fear hurts people directly

when friends aren't allowed to come over and play,

when stores and opportunities disappear,

when people are prevented from connecting with each other.

1

It's about who instills fear in others and you.

And it's about who has the privilege of being afraid.

And the toll your fears have on others.

This is also a book about the defaults.

It's about the exaggerations and (in)visibility that are the stuff of defaults.

It's about how the defaults hurt others and you.

It's about being curious enough to (un)learn the defaults.

This is a book about conversations and connections.

About the connections we miss because of segregation.

About the conversations we don't have because we miss the connections.

Or because we're afraid (see above).

About the conversations we do have that can nudge new connections.

And about the people who are curious enough to have them.

This is a book about being in the wrong place at the wrong time.

And about putting ourselves in the right place.

This is a book about how actions

can change the default

break the barricades

expose and move past the fear.

This is a book about the ripple effect of mundane warnings and the butterfly effect of little nudges.

This is a book about apathy, sympathy, and empathy.

This is a book about saviors, tourists, defenders, messengers, ambassadors, and accomplices.

TONIKA GNELL LEWIS

BIRTHDATE:	November 12, 1979
HEIGHT:	48"
WEIGHT:	52 lbs
EYE COLOR:	Dark Brown
HAIR COLOR:	Black
CLOTHING SIZE:	6
SHOE SIZE:	12-1/2
PHOTO DATE:	March 14, 1986

SAG

TONIKA'S STORY

OR AS LONG AS I CAN REMEMBER, I HAVE BEEN SURROUNDED by art and artists. If you walked through my home when I was a little girl, you'd see my mom writing a script, my grandma singing and playing piano, my uncles working on paintings and me smiling in front of my dad's ever-present camera. Art was normalized as a career choice in my family. All I had to do was pick my medium. Even after my parents divorced when I was a toddler, I still lived in my grandma's 2-flat with my mom, my grandma, and my uncles all in the same building. A typical day in my childhood included laughing with my favorite uncle, hugs from my grandma, and riding a bike to the corner store with my friends. My dad lived nearby, and I still saw him (and his camera) frequently. I still have a scar on my face from when my best friend Raymond and I tried to climb up a tree on one of our neighborhood adventures and I fell on a gate.

I grew up in Englewood, a neighborhood on the South Side of Chicago. According to the Census, Englewood's population consisted of 48,244 Black residents and 190 White residents in 1990. Multi-generational living was the rule in my neighborhood. Books and magazines were constant companions. I attended Englewood's Gershwin Elementary school in first grade, where I loved going to the assemblies in the auditorium where we did poetry readings and little shows. When I was seven, my mom and I moved to an apartment on the North Side, and I went to a public school there in third grade. Then my mom enrolled me in a Catholic school that was near her job. We took the train together every morning and then my mom would pick me up for our train ride back home after school. I was addicted to Dr. Seuss, then Shel Silverstein, then R.L. Stine's Fear Street series, and of course the Baby-Sitters Club series. It tickles me to remember how many times I re-read 20,000 Leagues Under the Sea. Then my grandma got sick when I was eleven and my mom and I moved back to Englewood to be with her. I continued to ride the train most days with my mom to the same Catholic school I attended when we lived on the North Side. One of my favorite shopping centers had disappeared by then and my friends from other neighborhoods were never allowed to come over to my house. I didn't know this at the time, but their parents thought it was too dangerous. Also, there were places I was told not to go. But I still had a great time. One of my favorite memories is reading hour in sixth grade, when an older White teacher named Ms. Hawkins would open the windows to let some fresh air in and give us lemonade while we took turns reading books like *Catcher in the Rye*. Reading is still one of my favorite things. My childhood was mostly magical, better than most. But when I tell people where I'm from, they usually ask just two questions (in one form or another) about my upbringing:

"How did you make it out?!" and/or "Have you ever seen a shooting?"

To be honest, I had no idea that I lived in the "poster child" of bad neighborhoods until I got to high school on the North Side. I remember telling other students where I was from and feeling so surprised when they said "oh my gosh! Are you ok?" I couldn't understand why they were acting like it was so bad to grow up where I grew up. I was a typical 13-year-old kid – I didn't watch the news.

Ever since that time, I've had to deal with people thinking that I must have been exposed to drugs and violence, that my childhood must have been awful, but it wasn't. In fact, my first and only encounter with the police as a child didn't happen in Englewood – it happened on the North Side when I was a sophomore in high school. Three of my Black high school friends and I were pulled over and frisked for no reason on the way to drop me off at my train stop after school. I did so well in grade school that I was accepted at Lane Tech, a prestigious selective enrollment public high school in the North Side neighborhood of Roscoe Village. The distance between my home and my high school was a little less than 15 miles, which might not sound that far, but for 13-year-old me, it was like traveling to another state; I caught a city bus every morning at 5:45, then transferred to a train, then to another city bus to arrive at school just in time for the 8:00 a.m. bell.

To be honest, I had no idea that I lived in the "poster child" of bad neighborhoods

As I listened to Common, Mobb Deep, Nas and Wu-Tang on my Walkman and stared out the bus window then the train window then the bus window each day, I couldn't help but notice how the neighborhoods changed even as the street names didn't. As we traveled north, I saw retail stores, all kinds of grocery stores, crosswalks, well-kept parks, playgrounds, and restaurants; and as we traveled back south, I noticed the lack of these resources and the abandoned lots and boarded up houses in my own neighborhood. I felt terrible when I realized that my neighborhood was ugly compared to the neighborhoods on the North Side. I was an artist. I couldn't help but see that. I started to feel the unfairness of it all. Even though all during my childhood, my family was always joking, arguing, and talking about Black social and political issues,

I didn't see the direct impact of racism on my neighborhood until I started traveling to Lane Tech. Over time my awareness of these issues grew, and I became determined to disrupt segregation with my art.

At the same time, I was exposed to the life-changing benefits of diversity at Lane Tech. Because the school is so highly rated, people from all over the city apply there to be one of the 4,000 students who score high enough on the entrance exams to attend. There were students with families from Puerto Rico, Philippines, Poland, Nigeria, Mexico, China, Haiti, Panama, Belize, Jamaica, and all over the world. This experience expanded my worldview, especially because we were just kids who weren't yet corrupted by the idea that we should know everything about each other or only socialize with our own "kind." We were curious and we made mistakes. We learned how to talk to each other by talking to each other. All of us said something offensive at one time or another because we didn't know the right way to say something about another culture. I had no idea that Chinese had many dialects, and Mandarin was the most common. I didn't know the difference between Puerto Rican and Mexican culture.

My dad's passion for photography was really helpful too. It was natural for me to take photos all the time and people felt so good when I took their picture – just like I did when my dad took pictures of me and my family. My photo-covered locker was like a "little museum of me and my friends kickin' it," according to my classmates. This was before the days of digital photography, so we were always excited when I got the negatives, laughing and looking forward to seeing the pictures.

One of my other favorite high school memories is the international food days – where students and their families would bring in food from their cultures and we could go to different booths and sample the food and talk. I loved learning about all the spices and the various ways that people cooked food. We learned all about the customs in different cultures by visiting each other in our homes. I mean sure you can go to a restaurant to taste food from all over the world, but that is nowhere near as good as sitting in someone's kitchen and having their mom or grandma cook a meal, seeing the spices they use and the stuff they keep in their refrigerator. I remember being so surprised that home-cooked Jamaican food tasted so much better than the restaurant versions I had tried. I had never even heard of Caribbean green soup, and I still love Belizean fry jacks.

I also loved sleepovers. Like most kids, I wanted to host friends at my house. My parents were fine with this, but my friends' parents would never let their kids come to my neighborhood. By the time I was five years old, I knew on some level that friends would never be able to come to my house in Englewood but I still invited them. I couldn't articulate what was happening at the time, but now I realize that I didn't have this core childhood experience of friends visiting my home and meeting my family and neighborhood friends. It wasn't until after I started high school that it dawned on me that this wasn't right, that something was messed up about the fact that if someone from my neighborhood wanted to host a graduation party or a sleepover, they had to rent a hotel room downtown. This still happens – parents are still afraid to let their kids come visit my kids in Englewood. This is a real shame, not only because it's so unfair to my kids, but also because I love to host and I'm proud of my home-cooking and having my kids' friends over is one of my favorite things too. I am raising my kids in Greater Englewood not because we are stuck, but because we love it here – the sense of family and community and the art, the resilience of this community – it's special. My childhood friend Raymond cuts my son's hair now. It doesn't get much better than that.

When I enrolled in a summer photography workshop after my freshman year in high school, I got my first real camera and became even more obsessed with the power of photography. After he had introduced me to the work of Black photographers who, like me, were passionate about capturing the beauty of everyday Black life in Black neighborhoods, my mentor Ovie Carter purchased a new camera and gave me his Nikon with all the lenses and the case. This was when I realized I had a chance at being taken seriously as a photographer – if someone like Ovie Carter bequeathed his camera to me, I must have been more than capable. Ovie Carter also told me I should major in photojournalism not photography in college, since I was already a good photographer and writing would make it possible for me to earn a living with my work.

But when I got to Columbia College, I learned about the standard career path for a young photojournalist. Step One: photograph crime – if it bleeds it leads. I have never wanted to invade someone's personal trauma in this way and obviously crime-centered photography makes it much harder to desegregate any city. Remember, pictures often say more about the photographer than the neighborhood – if you think you'll run into trouble, you're gonna see evidence of trouble. In essence, photojournalism was a euphemism for crime-centered photography, especially in my neighborhood. I can remember thinking – ah, so this is why my high school friends couldn't come over to my house, this is why they gasped in horror when I told them where I lived. Also, while I do love to write, photography has always been my preferred medium. To combat the crime-centered narrative that keeps resources and people away from Englewood, I was determined to show people the everyday beauty I witnessed in my community. In 2008, I created my first social justice photography project, Everyday Englewood.

By 2011, I was tired of waiting for the city of Chicago to address the inequity in Englewood, so I cofounded RAGE, the Residents Association of Greater Englewood, to empower the residents to act with or without the support of city hall. From April 2017 to April 2018, my photography from Everyday Englewood was the centerpiece of a monthly rotation of Englewood images featured on five billboards in my neighborhood. My work has been displayed at many cultural and civic locations, including the Chicago Cultural Center, the Harold Washington Library, and the Loyola University Museum of Art (LUMA). In 2017, I was named a Chicagoan of the Year by *Chicago Magazine*.

In 2016, I had been inspired by the idea of folding a map of Chicago in half and taking pictures of mirrored locations on the South and North Sides – for example, I would take photos of 6900 North Ashland and 6900 South Ashland. I also filmed videos of streets in corresponding neighborhoods on the South and North Sides to show people the inequity I had seen on those bus and train rides in high school. As I took pictures of homes, residents came out and asked me what I was doing. When I told them, they asked questions and engaged me in conversations. By that time, I saw photography as a window, invaluable just as it is, but now I wanted to open that window and listen in. I wanted to step into the lives of the people in these houses, introduce them to each other, and show Chicagoans that yes, it is possible to cross the invisible lines created by segregation. I filmed these conversations on location at the residents' homes. I was determined to portray Englewood residents and their homes with dignity to further combat the negative view of my neighborhood. We weren't stuck.

I wanted to step into the lives of the people in these houses, introduce them to each other, and show Chicagoans that yes, it is possible to cross the invisible lines created by segregation

We were resilient, creative, connected, and determined to get the resources we were entitled to.

I interviewed "map twins" (people who lived at the same-numbered buildings on the North and South ends of the same street) and asked them five simple questions: How did you come to live in your neighborhood? How would you describe your neighborhood? Is everything that you need on a day-to-day basis accessible in your neighborhood and, if not, what's missing? Is your place of peace in your neighborhood? How much did your house cost or how much do you pay for rent? South Siders were largely shocked by the price of homes in more affluent neighborhoods and North Siders were confronted by things like the lack of grocery stores in Englewood and even more by the fact that as North Siders, they were enjoying the benefits of federal, state, and municipal policies and resources that were not also being provided for their map twin, someone they were getting to know, someone who was also paying their fair share of taxes. Laws and policies are important, but if we really want to disrupt segregation, we have to get to know each other. I wanted all of us to realize what we have in common and become curious about our differences – I want us to care about each other.

These videos became a central feature of the multi-media interactive art installation that became Folded Map – the project that brought Maria and me together. From the minute I met her, I felt like we had twin brains – she's just as passionate as I am about dismantling segregation and she loves diving right in and getting things done. Maria knows she can count on me, and I know I can count on her. Without her amazing ability to organize things and see the sociology, this book would not have happened. I am sure of it. And you know, our friendship is a disruption to segregation too. I mean, who would have thought that a White academic and a Black social justice artist would become Folded Map besties?

MARIA'S STORY

IN 1968, MY FAMILY AND I MOVED TO BROOKINGS, SOUTH Dakota, home of South Dakota State University and the USDA Northern Grains Insect Research Laboratory, which utilizes the vast tracts of farmland surrounding the town to conduct research about soil, crop, and pest management services. I was two years old. My father was a research entomologist for the USDA and an amateur photographer. My mother, a potter who traveled to summer art fairs to sell her practical wares, was one of the original founders of the Brookings Summer Arts Festival. I loved serving as her little cashier at art fairs in the summertime, and I remember a run on the quiche pans she made in the 1970s. I also loved pestering my dad. If you were to walk to the top of the basement stairs in my childhood home, you might hear my mom operating her pottery wheel or firing up her kiln, along with my dad's gruff response to my persistent pleas for entry to his darkroom. "No. I can't open the door." If you were there when he finally let me in, you'd hear my dad's gruff response once again as I pleaded for escape – once my eyes adjusted to the darkness, I realized there wasn't all that much to see. Even so, my habit of knocking on that door continued for quite some time. I kept thinking that there must be something worthwhile, that I must be missing something. Maybe this is the same nagging sensation that has kept me persistently seeking answers to my questions about segregation and pushed me to find alternative ways to think about my scholarly work. Much the same way as the photography class I took in college helped me see photography as an art form, not just a "memory catcher."

In 1970, of the 13,717 people living in Brookings, three were Black

To state the obvious, Brookings is very small. I think I was in middle school when the first McDonalds was built there. Brookings is also predominantly, overwhelmingly, White. According to the Census, in 1970, of the 13,717 people living in Brookings, three were Black. The railroad tracks right behind our house accommodated freight trains which ran through twice a day. There was no need for passenger trains, buses, cabs or any public transportation. Brookings airport accommodated small prop planes, not passenger jets. When I was in high school, my mother went back to graduate school for her Master of Arts degree in English, and she worked at the Waldenbooks Store in the shopping mall, which was conveniently located across the tracks behind my house. The two grade schools, one middle school and one high school in my town were free public schools, which offered above average academic curriculums as well as robust sports and music programs. Like the town, my schools were almost entirely White. Not only were there no Black students in my 187-student graduation class in 1984 – there were none at all in the entire high school at the time. There were two Black students when I was in elementary school – they were siblings who lived with their adoptive White family. But they moved to another town after just a few years in Brookings. My two older brothers and I probably could have walked the two miles to our elementary school (or, later, the one mile to our high school), but we were more likely to ride bikes. And usually my parents would drive us; the weather in South Dakota is rarely not inclement between Fall and Spring.

I was not a rebel. I played clarinet in the band and in our school's two musicals – *Fiddler on the Roof* and *Man of La Mancha*. I also played saxophone in the marching and jazz bands, swam competitively, and I was a diehard member of the theater crew. I pounded more nails and washed more paint brushes than you can imagine. And there's more. I played on the freshman basketball team before I shifted to tennis, and I studied hard. I was a straight A student. One of my favorite things to do was lie on my bed and read books. I loved Laura Ingalls Wilder and *Little House on the Prairie* of course, but I hated Nancy Drew. She was way too serious – Bobbsey Twins and Trixie Belden were more my style. (Even though I was a geek, I had a lot of fun.) My family's social life centered around swimming (my brothers and I were all on the town's swim team – me from age 5 to 16), and many of our weekends were spent traveling to swim meets during the school year and camping with other swim families in the summer. Frankly, there weren't that many ways to get into trouble where I lived. I never wanted to drink or do drugs, so the most trouble we got into was when cops from three jurisdictions busted us for hopping the fence into a football field. I was terrified when they chased us down. We got stopped for things like running into a Dairy Queen parking lot after closing hours on a scavenger hunt but, once the cops realized we weren't drinking, they let us move on. We were oddballs who thought it was fun to do things like figure out how to make fortune cookies and celebrate Chinese New Year in May.

I would never say I didn't see race because I am a White person who was raised in North America. Everyone here sees race. But race wasn't a big topic of conversation in Brookings. I don't really remember when I first thought about what I thought about Black people. The mother of one of my friends taught at the boarding school for Native Americans in a town outside Brookings, and she was probably the first person who talked to me about concrete examples of inequity and social injustices. I'll always remember the first time she called me "plucky." I thought maybe she was making fun of my physique and when I got home, I looked up the word in the dictionary. I was relieved to see that plucky means brave, feisty, or spirited.

After high school, I attended Stanford University in California. I thought since I aced math in high school all the way through trigonometry, I should probably make math my major. On the first day of calculus, I had to ask someone what AP meant when the professor told us that since most of us had taken pre-calculus as AP students, we were going to jump right past the basics. (AP, I learned, stands for Advanced Placement.) I didn't even know what calculus was. I still don't and after one terrible quarter, I flirted with switching my major to English for a few quarters. I don't remember any "aha" moment that caused me to declare sociology as my ultimate major, which I did after returning from a quarter studying overseas in France my junior year. As I progressed through my sociology classes, I did wonder what race consciousness about Black people looks like in a town like Brookings (it was pretty clear to me what was going on with Native Americans, since we lived in South Dakota, home of nine Indian Reservations, including some of the largest in the country). What does someone who grew up in a town like mine think about Black people? I knew I wasn't a blank slate – no one is, but I really had no conscious ideology about race besides the conversations with my friend's mom about the boarding school. I did think about those conversations while I was in college, and for a time I wanted to use my sociology degree to return to South Dakota and do something about the injustices perpetrated against Native Americans.

I returned to South Dakota to work as a lifeguard during the summers, and I stayed with my parents in Yakima, Washington one summer for an internship in social work. That's when I learned that my passion for sociology did not translate into a passion for being a social worker. Since there really weren't many opportunities in South Dakota when I graduated in 1988, I ended up moving to Washington DC. There, I shared a house with three friends and worked as a research assistant for Child Trends and also did part-time work for the American Sociological Association. Those experiences helped me decide that I did want to get a PhD and that I liked doing research. So I moved to Ann Arbor, Michigan, to get my PhD. I knew I wanted to study race, and serendipity stepped in to help me decide exactly what I wanted to focus on. The professor (Reynolds Farley), who was an author on a famous journal article in 1978 ("Chocolate City, Vanilla Suburbs: Will the trend toward racially separate communities continue?") that I had read as an undergraduate, was replicating the study and needed a graduate assistant. I ended up working with a racially diverse team of graduate students who went on to have careers studying race in America. After earning my PhD in 1996, I worked at Penn State for four years and then decided I wanted to move out of Happy Valley in 2000. That year I got an offer to work at University of Illinois Chicago (UIC).

By then, I was a sociologist who studied residential segregation, so I had read about Oak Park and how the people there had worked to create a racially integrated community, starting in the 1960s, when White flight was rampant in the Chicago area. My close friend Ellen also lived in Oak Park, and so I set out to find a place to live, with her as my sounding board. I called Ellen when I found an apartment in Oak Park near Austin Boulevard (the dividing line between Oak Park and Chicago) and, among other things, she assured me that it was safe. When I think about it, I could just have easily called another colleague who would have told me: "Oh, you definitely shouldn't live so close to Austin Boulevard." I'm not sure if I would have made a different choice. I like to think I wouldn't have. But who knows? I stayed in that apartment for two years, and then I bought a condo right on Austin Boulevard in Oak Park, before buying my current home in Galewood, a racially diverse community on the northwest side of Chicago. At the time of this writing, I have been a sociologist at UIC for more than 20 years.

About 12 years ago, I "met" a resident from Englewood for the first time (as far as I know) during a research project designed to gather personal perceptions about neighborhoods in Chicago. As a sociologist I knew how valuable it was to understand race through questions about place. This is because (1) in talking about places, we could see racial attitudes acted out in real life – decisions about where to live or visit – rather than a box checked on a survey; and (2) people seemed more comfortable talking about race through the lens of place. By that, I mean that White people were more honest about race when talking about places – in my experience Black people are not as uncomfortable talking about race.

All summer long, from behind a two-way mirror, I observed one-on-one interviews between my graduate student assistants and Latinx, Black, and White Chicago residents. My research team and I were exposed to the media's obsession with Englewood's crime. And several interviewees described their "harrowing" experiences of "ending up" in Englewood after taking a wrong turn. Even though none of them were subjected to violence, anger, or even mild disrespect during their "encounters" with Englewood residents, the interviewees unanimously expressed fear, and sympathy for the "unfortunate" people who "had" to live in the neighborhood.

When we showed the interviewees a map of Chicago, almost all of the White people (and some of the Black people) pointed to Englewood as "a place they would never live." When we asked why, we received variants of "the place is just horrible." Even a White Chicagoan who knew absolutely nothing about any of the other locations on the map of Chicago somehow knew all about the dangerous conditions in that neighborhood, Englewood.

So when one of our interviewees answered our first question "Where do you live?" by checking the box that indicated Englewood, we felt like we'd just met someone famous. Because of a childcare emergency, she arrived for her interview with three small children in tow. We quickly found some kid-worthy snacks and engaged a friendly staff member to stay with the children in another room while my research assistant conducted the interview, and I observed from behind the two-way mirror. Until this moment, the woman fit the "sociological profile" of Englewood residents who experience the very real challenges of being a single Black mother with a low income, but she did not even come close to the stereotypical category of poor people in constant despair. She was attending college to make a better life for herself, and her family, and she was determined to succeed. To describe the interview results anonymously, I created pseudonyms. For this mother of three, I chose the name Destiny because I was struck by her singular determination to make her dreams come true. In essence, Destiny's interview personalized and humanized Englewood residents for me and for all the students involved in the research project. (Up to that point, our only "data" were the misperceptions and fear expressed by our other Chicago-area residents.) Years later, the content of these interviews became a part of my co-authored book, *Cycle of Segregation*.

In essence, Destiny's interview personalized and humanized Englewood residents for me and for all the students involved in the research project

I was a Stanford graduate, a sociologist who had spent her career utilizing surveys and interviews to understand the causes of residential segregation. I knew how to conduct sophisticated surveys and interview studies to unpack racial attitudes and dissect the processes responsible for segregation. I was starting to get better at framing the results of sociological research for audiences who don't read scholarly journal articles and who are seeking to change laws and policies that perpetuate segregation. All laudable and important work. But I wanted to figure out a way to directly impact people's lives. To expose the systems I had been studying to the people most touched by them in a way that inspired individual action. Looking back, I can imagine Destiny's interview as the warm ember just waiting to be sparked in 2018 right after *Cycle of Segregation* was published. Within a few months of my book coming out, several journalists called me to get the wonky sociologist's perspective about an exhibit:

"Have you ever heard of Folded Map?"

I hadn't.

But remember, I'm plucky.

THE STORY OF *DON'T GO* – TONIKA + MARIA'S STORY

Tonika: IN THE MONTHS BEFORE MEETING MARIA, I LEFT MY job as the sole Black woman on the executive team of a White majority nonprofit after being passed over for the role of director. The organization's leadership offered the role to my White colleague who had less experience than me. In fact, I had trained her when she joined the organization. When she got the job offer, she immediately told me and together we devised a plan to find a new director. Once that task was complete, both of us resigned. I had garnered renown as a social justice artist in the city of Chicago, but that did not alleviate the impact of more than a decade of microaggressions and racism in my nonprofit executive life. Even though I'm a relentless optimist, my experiences at work had left me feeling like the White world outside of my circle of friends and family was never going to validate my vision – they would always see me as less than because I was a Black woman from Englewood.

Maria: By the time I met Tonika, I had reached the top of the tenure ladder as a full professor, but I wanted to do something different. Something was missing. Authoring research studies that show the seemingly endless ways that segregation cycles through our lives had made me cynical. Sometimes, I thought of good, small ideas about how to break through the barriers of segregation, but I kept them to myself. My work demanded that I stay focused on the macro – that I propose ideas about institutional changes, not personal breakthroughs. I was starting to feel like I was going to end up a grumpy old professor!

When I started receiving phone calls from journalists two months before Folded Map was first exhibited to the public, I did not need to see the exhibit to recognize its conversation-changing nature. As soon as I heard about it, my sociological brain tuned into the fact that Tonika was (1) asking academic questions in plain language, (2) transforming sociological theories into relatable examples of segregation's direct, personal impact on everyday people every day, and (3) laying out a pathway for regular people to do something about segregation.

I knew that Tonika was onto something that I wouldn't have dreamt possible. This project was a way to move sociological practice out of the ivory tower and into the streets, in a way that could help shift people's perspective.

Tonika: When I saw the quote in an article about Folded Map in the *Chicago Tribune* – from "Maria Krysan, a University of Illinois at Chicago professor who wrote a book about the issue," I was floored! An academic author was talking about my project? I felt the same way I did when my mentor, Ovie Carter, bequeathed his Nikon to me; if a photographer like Ovie thought I was worthy of attention, maybe I really was a photographer who would be taken seriously. And if an academic like Maria thought Folded Map merited attention, maybe my art would be taken seriously as a social justice project.

After a few email exchanges, we agreed to meet for brunch at a café on the South Side. About 60 seconds after we sat down and settled Maria's 11-year-old daughter in with a stack of books to read, we got to work. As we worked together on the Folded Map Action Kit and other projects, we grew more and more passionate. Our twin brains melded into one when the post about

my presentation garnered the attention of Mary Schmich. Now, both of us were floored – a column about Folded Map by a Pulitzer Prize-winning columnist had gone viral in Chicago. By now, I had a large following on Instagram, so I set up a Gmail account and posted a request saying "send me your Don't Go stories."

Maria: More than 70 people responded within a few days. As a sociologist who routinely recruits interviewees for research projects, I'd never seen anything like this. I was riveted by the shapes and sizes of stories sent in by people from so many different areas and professions. Some were complete stories; others were snippets. A million sociology questions popped into my head: What can these stories reveal about the origin of our perceptions of the "South Side"? How do these messages help perpetuate segregation? And where do they come from? How do people overcome these messages? Tonika and I both knew that (a) we had struck a chord with Chicagoans and (b) there was an important artistic and social scientific story to be told.

I busily wrote a grant application (thank you to UIC for providing funding) and started filling in all the blanks like a dutiful sociologist. I drafted a protocol and started organizing the 70 or so emails so that I could come up with a strategy to figure out which people we wanted to talk to more. And I finally had a solid understanding of a role I could play to support Tonika's amazing work: she told me she was worried from the beginning that as a Black woman, there might be issues with her interviewing the primarily White people who shared their stories.

I nodded knowingly in response to her concern, "yup, race of interviewer effects. Check. I'm on it. I'm your girl. I'll interview the White people, and you can interview the people of color."

But before we could hit send on our first interview request, the pandemic hit and the sociological methods book was thrown out the window.

Where to do the interviews? Forget traveling, we're in lockdown. As with everything else in life, we thought, "what the heck, let's try Zoom," even though sociological methods books would warn against this – impersonal, harder to get people to open up, etc., etc. – but we really had no choice.

How to convince people to talk to us? Lots of people are stuck at home; it's the perfect time to try this out.

Race of interviewer effects? Still a worry.

So we emailed five of the people who had sent us a story, got responses from four of them, and scheduled our first interview with Tom on April 8, 2020. And by we, I mean we. Forget race of interviewer effects, I was insecure enough that I thought, whatever we might lose, we have to do this first one together, so I know what Tonika is after.

Two or three interviews later, it was clear that

(1) Tonika had the star power, and all our storytellers would be disappointed if I showed up to interview them by myself (although Jerry, a sociologist, was actually wowed by yours truly – the one person out of 25 who thought Maria was cool);

(2) I needed to throw out my carefully crafted protocol – because Tonika was introducing ideas and topics and approaches that I never would have thought of, and any forced modification would have hampered the power of the interviews;

(3) Zoom interviews are awesome because a click of a button and we're all in a room (no Chicago traffic to deal with), the interview is being recorded (audio AND video), and we have a transcript within minutes;

(4) Race of interviewer effects? Forget about it; there was too much to learn and too much magic that came out of the alchemy between the Black woman and the White woman who were exploring these issues. Together. And this was primarily because:

(5) Tonika could get anybody to open up; our basic interview protocol was: Don't Go. Tell us about that.

Tonika: Maria handled all the sociology research duties to keep us on track – she scheduled the interviews, organized all the video recordings and transcripts, and sent reminders to participants (and me). We had finished 10 interviews when the country exploded with anti-racist marches in late May. Our mission of finishing this project seemed more important than ever. So, during that perfect storm of awfulness (aka 2020), we decided that the best way for us to fight racism was to continue with our *Don't Go* interviews. We finished our last interview in July of 2020.

Then Maria reviewed the videos and the transcripts, pulled out themes and important ideas for the stories, and created an initial structure for the book. Neither of us wanted to create some kind of sociological report or academic analysis. Both of us recognized the power of these stories, so we enlisted the help of a creative writer, Mary Gustafson, to keep the stories conversational and informal.

> They tell the story of the Don't Go messages, the people who send, upend, and get hurt by them. And importantly, they tell the stories of everyday people who disrupt segregation in all kinds of everyday ways

Maria and I agreed on four themes: Fear, Messengers, Shortcuts, and From Hurt to Healing. They tell the story of the Don't Go messages, the people who send, upend, and get hurt by them. And importantly, they tell the stories of everyday people who disrupt segregation in all kinds of everyday ways. And what the careful reader will notice – and what was a source of tremendous consternation for the sociologist (but neither me, the artist, nor

Mary, the writer) – is that all of the stories have something of each theme in them. So the thematic designation is a bit arbitrary. But of course it also reflects the reality: life is messy. And the stories are complicated.

I think the power of these stories is in large part due to the fact that Maria and I were both in a Zoom room. As a Black woman from Englewood who had so many diverse experiences, I was able to empathize with the people from Englewood and other disinvested communities. And I think White people were more comfortable with me because I really wanted to hear about their journey. I was fascinated – and I wanted to learn how they came into their stereotypical beliefs about Black people and Black neighborhoods and then how they overcame that conditioning. And by the end of that first interview, Maria and I were delighted. Maria, the former worried-about-becoming-a-grumpy-old-professor, was sharing her authentic reactions and experiences as a White person, not just as a sociologist. I mean, neither of us could ignore the fact that whatever we were doing, it was working.

The Setting

Chicago was 31% White, 29% Black, 30% Latino, and 7% Asian in 2020. It has the second largest population of Black people in the country (behind only New York City).

In 2020, Chicago also had the highest level of segregation between Black and White residents of all of our nation's big cities.

And Chicago has been segregated like that for decades, and over the past 40 years, progress has been minimal.

Researchers measure segregation by calculating the "Index of Dissimilarity." This number can vary from 0 (lowest segregation) to 100 (highest segregation). In 1980, Chicago's Index of Dissimilarity was 91. Four decades later, this number sits not much lower, at 80. To understand what this means, it can be helpful to think of the numbers as percentages of the populations that would have to move to create a city where people are evenly distributed (in proportion to their population size) throughout the city. So

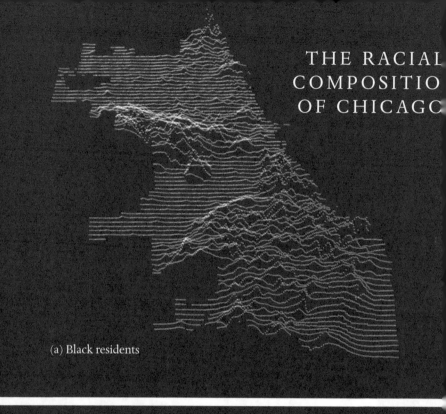

THE RACIAL
COMPOSITIO
OF CHICAGC

(a) Black residents

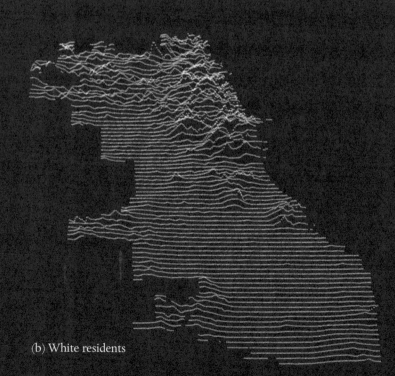

(b) White residents

(c) Hispanic residents

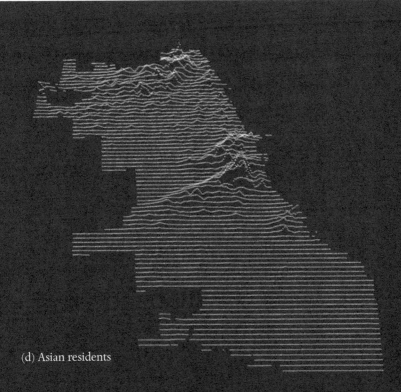

(d) Asian residents

today, 80% of the Black people or the White people in Chicago would need to move to get a score of "0."[2]

Most researchers agree that an Index of Dissimilarity over 60 is "very high." And even though Chicago is the worst big city (the fifth worst if you include the suburbs) in the United States, there is a close race to the bottom with New York, Detroit, Newark, Milwaukee, Gary, Cleveland, Philadelphia, St. Louis, Miami, and other cities. This is a race that no one wants to win of course – the higher the number, the worse the prognosis.

Where you live matters. It impacts both the access to and the quality of schools, jobs, health care, grocery stores, pharmacies, clothing stores, entertainment venues, childcare options, social services, recreational facilities, green spaces, crosswalks, street-lights, environmental hazard-free zones, and low crime rates. Honestly, we could fill this page with resources that are entirely dependent on where you live.[3]

And where you live – in Chicago and most cities across the country – is greatly dependent on race. Scores of academic reports and studies show us that segregation translates into racially distinct experiences. Separate is not equal. Not by a long stretch.

See for yourself. Go ahead and review the following statistics about two neighborhoods located on the maps that follow: Englewood and Lakeview.[4] Do you notice anything about the relationship between race and resources?

The racial composition maps that opened this section make it easy to see Chicago's segregation. It's not subtle, is it? You could say it's Black, White, and Brown. The population on the South and West Sides is predominantly Black; most of the White people live on the North Side while Latinx people make up most of the population in Northwest and Southwest Chicago neighborhoods.

Chicago's street system is a grid. That's why so many Chicagoans don't like to drive outside of the city – it's confusing out there. In Chicago, the same street can stretch for miles from the south side all the way to the north side of the city. To create a visual depiction of segregation's impact, Tonika folded her map along Madison Street – the center point where the street addresses flip from north to south.

But in Chicago, north and south are more than just designations on street signs or mailing labels. In less than one week, newcomers to Chicago pick up those ubiquitous local phrases that describe so much more than location: "the North Side" and "the South Side." Someone tells new arrivals about a new store that opened in the "North Side neighborhood of Rogers Park." Or about the school that's located in the "South Side neighborhood of Auburn Gresham." And eventually, maybe a couple weeks later, you'll start to hear about "the West Side" too. The East Side is trickier – Lake Michigan kind of gets in the way – although technically there is an East Chicago. But North, South, and West are the constant labels that not only contain geographic meanings, but also, and importantly, tremendous sociological, cultural, and economic meanings. But you don't have to take our word for it – this entire book is about the social significance of these labels – the codewords embedded in them – and the way in which they are used as tools of segregation.

And, before getting into the stories themselves, I (Maria) am occupationally obligated as a sociologist to provide a glimpse into what caused and continues to cause residential segregation. Literally thousands of articles, books, and reports have been written on this topic. So anything I write is necessarily an oversimplification.[5] And this is a book about stories, not about theories. (Even though, for the record, the stories fit very neatly into many of the theories.) I know you want to read the stories, not the theories. But here's a cheat sheet just in case:

(1) For decades, racist policies and practices at the local, state, federal, and industry level have cemented segregation into our city (and many other cities throughout the country). Think redlining,

Englewood

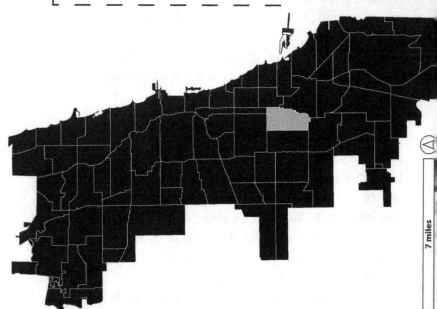

🏦	1	Number of banks
🍴	14	Number of restaurants
🛒	2	Number of grocery stores
🎓	9%	Percent of population with at least a Batchelor's degree
💵	$21,981	Median household income
🏠	$144,333	Median home price
🏘	24%	Percent of owner occupied housing
🏚	32.3%	Percent vacant housing units

Total population: 22,019
Race/ethnicity breakdowns:

Black/AA alone (92%)

Latino (4%)

Other (2%)

White alone (1%)

Asian (1%)

7 miles

Lakeview

🏦 **30**   Number of banks

🍴 **294**   Number of restaurants

🛒 **8**   Number of grocery stores

🎓 **83%**   Percent of population with at least a Bachelor's degree

🏠 **$90,401**   Median household income

🏦 **$480,977**   Median home price

🏘 **37%**   Percent of owner occupied housing

🔺 **7.6%**   Percent of vacant housing units

Total population: 101,428
Race/ethnicity breakdowns:

White alone (76%)		
Latino (9%)	Asian alone (7%)	Black/AA alone (4%)
		Other (4%)

7 miles

public housing siting, highway construction, racially restrictive covenants, blockbusting, land sale contracts, the list goes on. These practices and policies laid the foundation for the separate and unequal places that define Chicago today. In other words, we socially engineered segregation. Some helpful laws have been enacted and some racist policies and practices have been forbidden and outlawed. But there are still practices and policies (zoning laws, steering, predatory lending, illegal discrimination) that keep us segregated.

(2) Also for decades, scholars have focused on three traditional explanations that affect segregation to varying degrees: discriminatory policies and practices, economic differences, and personal preferences. People are often surprised to know that economic differences are not the biggest driver of segregation, that preferences people hold about who they want to share their neighborhood (racially speaking) with are more complicated than they assume, and discrimination, despite being illegal, is still with us.

(3) More recently, attention has been directed at some hidden-in-plain-sight factors that influence how people end up living where they do. Friends, family, and acquaintances influence what we know of places. We travel – or don't – through certain parts of the city as we go to work or school or play. The media – traditional and untraditional alike – paint pictures (usually not complete) of neighborhoods. In a segregated city, segregation begets segregation – our social networks tend to be segregated; our lived experiences differ based on our race, and the messages sent by the media are racialized. So the information and perceptions of communities, and the opportunities we have – which flow from our resources, preferences, and the barriers put up (or not put up) by discrimination – end up funneling us into the silos of segregated neighborhoods.

Some Basic Details about the Interviews

Our interviews were conducted in 2020, and this book is being published in 2025. Many of our storytellers have had events happen in their lives in the four years it has taken us to publish this book. When we connected with them again, they gave us permission to refrain from updating their stories, as we wanted a time capsule. We wanted to capture how they felt about the issues at the time of their interviews. But as you can imagine, especially given the thoughtfulness of each of our storytellers, several of them would say things differently now; would have more stories to tell; and would have more reflections to share. But that can be for another day.

We interviewed a total of 29 people during this project; this book includes 25 of their stories: 17 women and 8 men. There are 17 White people, 3 Black people, 2 multi-racial people, 1 Latinx person, 1 Hispanic,* and 1 Asian person. Two of the storytellers are first-generation immigrants. The interviews were conducted between April 8 and July 22, 2020 – 10 before the end of May and the racial protests surrounding George Floyd's murder, and 15 after.

Our respondents ranged in age from 20-somethings to almost 60-somethings (but mostly 30- and 40-somethings). The storytellers include educators, artists, social workers, nonprofit leaders, graphic designers, engineers, piano technicians, small business owners, advocates, community organizers, and others.

The interviews lasted about an hour, and in a few cases, we had follow-up interviews. For all but one, who preferred a pseudonym for personal reasons, we refer to our storytellers by their real first names.

---

* This represents one storyteller who is an immigrant from Spain, who, based on the US Census definitions, is Hispanic, while the term Latinx is for those born in the Americas.

In 2021, Block Club Chicago, a nonprofit news service in Chicago, published five stories from this project, and the response and reactions solidified our intuition: these stories had to be told.

The Raw Data

We got more than 70 responses in the "Don't Go" email inbox. They ranged from a few words ("I've got some stories to tell you!") to a few pages. Together we knew we had something powerful in these "raw data." And the Zoom conversations we had with the email writers resulted in many hours of fascinating, funny, and heart-wrenching conversations. But sometimes, the raw data speak volumes more than any distillation or excavation can. This was true of the first story we're sharing with you. We are letting Emily's initial email response speak for itself.

"Dear Tonika,

I saw the clip you posted with the group of NU students (I follow you on IG and FB) and I just read Mary's column in the Trib. As I'm sure many folks have expressed, it didn't surprise me at all that local college kids are warned not to head south. I sort of understand the apprehension – a teenager comes to a big city for school and is given advice by their families/friends/schools about where to go/not go and what to do/not do. Those giving the advice are likely basing it on the little they know, which probably comes from crime reports, news stories, so-and-so's sister who lived there once, etc. Still, one would hope these kids venture out, push some boundaries (figuratively and literally), and explore all parts of the city.

I'm a bit more disheartened by the folks who actually live in Chicago or the close suburbs. Unfamiliarity seems to breed fear. Again, news stories and crime reports are generally all they know about certain neighborhoods and folks will likely remember a negative story even if they're also exposed to positive stories about a neighborhood (which themselves are rare). Fear is powerful.

I went to an all-girls high school right at the city border. Most of my classmates were from working class South Side families, many first-generation Americans. I spent much of my childhood visiting my mom's relatives in Roseland and Pullman until most of them either moved away or passed away, circa the early 1990s. Then I moved to Rogers Park for college and have been there ever since.

I still go down to Pullman/Roseland regularly – house tours, restaurant excursions, drive-bys to check on my grandmother's old house, Old Fashioned Donuts (!!) and, most recently, breakfast at The Ranch Steakhouse. I have a real fondness for the area because I spent so much time there as a kid.

I agree with Mary Schmich (and you) that all it takes is a trip to one restaurant, one park, one festival to dispel those dumb fears and start the familiarity process. I wish more people would take the time to venture out. The South Side is so huge, so diverse, so fascinating, with so much history. It drives me bonkers that so many people are missing out on more than *half* of their city.

One other tidbit – I've sometimes looked at the postings of former residents of Pullman/Roseland on FB, lamenting on how their beloved childhood neighborhoods are in such bad shape and how sad they are at how the neighborhood has 'changed' (code word, of course).

And all I can think is, well,

you abandoned your neighborhood.

You could have stayed,

you could have welcomed a new neighbor who might not look like you,

you could have embraced a little diversity on your block.

But instead,

you White-flighted right out of there.

One last random memory – when I was in late high school, I think, I attended an event somewhere in the city where a friend was working (music fest, I think?) and I was chatting with a White kid who wasn't from Chicago (can't recall if he was a suburban kid or out-of-stater) and when I said where I was from, his response was something along the lines of,

'Wait, what? There are *White* people on the South Side!?!' Sigh. Keep up the good work, Tonika!

–Emily

P.S. I've attached a photo of me and my brother and cousin on the porch of our Noni's house in Pullman."

Section 1
Fear

GRANDMA'S NO-GO ZONE –
ADRIANNE'S STORY

I DEBATED CONTACTING TONIKA BECAUSE IT'S SHAMEFUL TO admit that I've been complicit, but I want to change, and change is uncomfortable.

Shortly after I bought my first car when I was 17, I drove down to see my grandma. She lives in a middle-class area of Chicago on the South Side called Beverly. I was a relatively new driver, and I got off at the wrong exit. We didn't have Google Maps or anything like that when I was young, and I didn't know where I was. So I called my grandparents to ask for directions.

They lost it. They said I was in a *very* dangerous place.

They were so freaked out for me. And then I got freaked out too. When I finally got to my grandparents' house, they were really mad. Later, I witnessed my cousin getting into big trouble for getting off at the wrong exit too. So I was really scared.

Now I'm 34 years old, and I had never, ever gone to any place on the South Side other than my grandma's house. It was deeply ingrained in me not to go. I was told that I could get hurt or shot or all of these terrible things if I left the safe bubble of my grandma's street.

I spent my childhood living "all around" predominantly White Chicago suburbs. After a two-year stint in San Francisco, I moved

back to Chicago's North Side as an adult and opened a storefront boutique and art studio in Ravenswood on the North Side. I named the store Ponnopozz after my two imaginary childhood friends, Ponno and Pozzer.

After George Floyd was murdered, I just could not keep posting my usual content. I thought, I have to let everybody who follows me know how I feel and how I'm going to work on these issues. As a business owner, I felt a responsibility to do something. Because a lot of the people who follow my art are like me, and they wouldn't say anything, or they would stay in their White privilege and not look at this. Because it's uncomfortable, because you know, we've never *had* to do *that*.

I was angry that I just blindly believed everything I was taught

So I started to get off the highway at places I was told to never, ever, go. It was not what I thought. It's just neighborhoods and nice homes. I was angry that I just blindly believed everything I was taught.

When businesses began to slowly reopen in the summer during the pandemic, I decided to open on Saturdays only. I planned to showcase art and products from a different Black or Brown artist each week. I wanted to spotlight them. I'm not taking a percentage of the sales. I did this specifically just to amplify artists I never amplify. This Saturday I am featuring my Latino friend. He's my first. But then honestly, I'm just taking whoever I know and putting them in here. I don't know that many.

And then, how would I ask them? I'm nervous about the wording. I grew up, you know, I'm a White person, we're taught that ALL LIVES MATTER. Color doesn't exist. To say something like, I'm specifically looking for a Black artist feels really uncomfortable.

I could see Black artists getting offended, thinking I only wanted them because they were Black or Brown. Or worse, they might see ME as trying to be a White savior.

Plus, would Black artists even be interested in showing their art on the North Side? Like will their art fit in with my vibe? Maybe Black artists won't fit in with the vibe of my neighborhood. Maybe people wouldn't understand the art or relate to it. Maybe none of the artist's fans would be interested in coming here!

The art I make is super fun and bubbly – maybe deeper art or things about cultural issues would not fit in.

The segregation in Chicago really angers me, but I felt helpless until I saw Tonika on Instagram, talking about little things you can do, like visiting new places or making new friends.

I drove directly into my grandma's no-go zone.
Only this time, no one was mad

A month or so later we followed up with Adrianne on another Zoom call because she wanted to report back on the conversation she had with her grandma about her burgeoning anti-racism efforts:

The conversation went much better than I thought it would. And after my interview with you, I remember thinking, "Oh good, I'll be able to showcase some new artists, maybe we can even be friends on social media." But I made real friends. One artist I met through Tonika actually invited me to her friend's birthday party, and to get there, I took the same wrong exit I took when I was 17.

I drove directly into my grandma's no-go zone.

Only this time, no one was mad.

ADVENTURES OF A WHITE DUDE – JERRY'S STORY

"ALL WHITES KNOW" – A POEM WRITTEN BY A WHITE DUDE named Jerry

Among us White folks
We all know there's neighborhoods we can't go
We all know we're not welcome in some spots
We all know what will happen if we go there

So I went there
And it's true
I've been assaulted. . . .
By my own thoughts
Am I supposed to be here?
Is everyone looking at me?
What do they think when they see me?

I've been shot at a few times . . .
Words flying out of their mouths like bullets
Of kindness
Like "Excuse me, you drop that?"
And "Ay, what's up?"
And "How you doing today?"
And "Damn, that's a nice ass beard."

But mostly
I've been confronted by gangs . . .
Of silence and apathy
No handshakes
No smiles that say "Thanks for gracing us with
Your presence"
Just folks going about their business
Like they should
Because I'm not a unicorn
And I'm not the enemy
I'm just a White dude walking through their
neighborhood.

I'm gonna do this! I am going to the South Side. Now, how long is the bus ride from Hyde Park to Englewood? Oh crap, it's an hour and 10 minutes?!?

I distinctly remember this trip as a University of Chicago graduate student in sociology, going to Englewood on the bus for the first time. I got on a packed bus, and I had a strong sense that I was this White dude on this bus of all Black people.

I had to get off the bus and stand at an intersection waiting for the next bus. Some of these buses can be 20 minutes apart and I had the sense of like,

"Here I am this White dude standing on Stony and 69th. And, you know, I must be standing out. And people must be wondering why I'm here. What I'm doing."

And when we talk about the scenarios where you hear you're unsafe, this was it!

You're not so worried about something happening to you on a bus, but a White dude standing on an intersection? I remember being like,

"Okay, when they say stuff happens, this is where it goes *down*. This is it. This is where it happens.

Text mama and tell her you love her!"

There was a corner store right across the street and there's a couple of dudes sitting out there. And I'm thinking, "This is it, it's about to go down."

But, I'm still here, you know? Turns out it's really uneventful.

And so, with nary a crime, my maiden 4-mile voyage from Hyde Park to the Kusanya coffee shop in Englewood came to an end. In fact, I lived to tell the tale and take more bus rides to the South Side. For a long time, I was like,

"These people got to be wondering, where am I going?

What do I need to be careful *not* to be doing?

You ask yourself a series of questions

am I standing in the way?

If the window seat is open, but somebody is sitting in the aisle seat, can I be like,

'Hey, excuse me, can I get into that window seat?'

Am I in the way?

Am I out of the way?

What do I do?

Just don't be a rude White dude!"

Eventually, I realized that the people on the bus weren't focused on me. They don't care.

Part of Whiteness seems to be that you think everybody gives a damn. Like you think that when you're in these spaces, Black folks can't help but be like,

"Oh, who is this guy? I wonder why *he's* here?"

But Black people have their own lives. They don't care why you're there. And they certainly don't care about you waiting for a bus. They don't care about you sitting on a bus. Seriously, you could write a Dr. Seuss book about this.

So I think we need to get into that kind of space and feel all the uncomfortableness and whatever. And to be really honest, I felt some shame. That even as an academic who'd been studying this stuff, I too was fearing things. I know I shouldn't be afraid, but I guess this is just part of the process. Apparently, just reading books doesn't change everything.

I kept trying to allow myself to feel all the feelings, while also trying to figure out what has to happen so that I don't feel this way anymore. Like, is this about repeatedly doing it? Will I get more comfortable the more I do this?

When I was in middle school in the 1990s, I remember overhearing my parents talking about how another family in the neighborhood had said they "weren't going to sell their home to no N-word" because they didn't want to have someone "'like that' living in their place."

I had Black classmates, so I was kind of baffled.

Me and my grade school friends did not understand that a reason to move would be because somebody Black is moving in nearby. Or even because lots of Black people were moving into the neighborhood. White flight is confusing to kids. But then overhearing these adult conversations, I was like,

"Man, this must be bad. It must be *really* bad. If this is what people are saying. If people are really leaving because Black people are moving in. Wow, this must be really serious."

I do remember my parents saying,

"We disagree with that kind of language. *We* don't use that around here."

They made it clear that those were not the views that we as a family ought to be holding. Which I think probably is part of the way that most White folks manage this stuff: *We* move for education. And *we're* not like *those* people.

So we moved from integrating Dolton, a small village just over the southern border of Chicago to all-White Dyer, a town in Indiana that's commonly considered to be a southern suburb of Chicago. In 2020, Dyer was barely 4% Black (and about 80% White) and Dolton was more than 90% Black.

I ended up going to middle school and high school in Indiana, with a lot of the other White folks from Dolton. Some of the people who left Dolton went to a neighboring high school, so I played against them in sports and stuff. I definitely remember people would use language like:

"We escaped the neighborhood!

That neighborhood went downhill."

And I remember other people being more explicit:

"The neighborhood got ruined.

They ruined the neighborhood!"

So I understood; the neighborhood we left went downhill. The old neighborhood went bad because the Black folks moved in.

I distinctly remember saying things like, "I don't see color."

I thought it was all about hard work, that people who thought things were about race were just making excuses for their situation.

After all, my dad was a high school graduate, but not a great student. My mother did three years of college, and got married very young – at 21, I think. Against the odds, my parents worked hard to make sure I went on to college and my siblings all went on to college. We didn't have a bunch of money. My parents kind of scraped by. My dad was unemployed for a while after he got laid off from the railroad. So there was a bootstrap narrative that we made it *despite* some tough challenges.

When I went to seminary in Orlando, I was taught by a man who was born in Mexico. Another one of my professors was a woman from Puerto Rico. For the first time, I had informed conversations about race, gender, and sexuality, and I realized that race affects everything. By the time I left this three-year program, I asked all kinds of questions and began to challenge the Christian faith I had grown up with.

I used to pray before every meal. I was thanking God for the food on the table one day when I thought, "Wait. Even in this country, there are people who don't have food on their table. There are hungry Black kids in America.

Why am I thanking this God for this food, when having access to this food is all about politics and economics and race?" This was in my mid-20s. That's when I really began to deconstruct the worldview I'd grown up with.

The professor who was born in Mexico put up with my ignorant White guy questions. He became a close friend and mentor to me. I also had a couple friends in seminary facing issues related to immigration status and green cards; I learned more about how the system works and what life was like for some of these folks.

I went on from seminary to earn my Master's degree in sociology. When I read about colorblind racism, I felt like they were talking about me. In my heart, I knew I saw color. Of course I did. I was never really "colorblind."

But then when I started my PhD program at the University of Chicago, I received clear messages from my peers:

"Don't go past the Midway!

Be careful.

Don't leave Hyde Park.

The South Side is *dangerous*!!"

So I decided to take that bus ride down to Englewood and see for myself. I just wanted to commit to trying to see what these spaces were like. And a little bit of me thought as a sociologist,

"Will I really put my money where my mouth is?

Am I gonna do this, or not?"

So I decided to take that bus ride down to Englewood and see for myself. I just wanted to commit to trying to see what these spaces were like. And a little bit of me thought as a sociologist, "Will I really put my money where my mouth is?"

I had to find alternative ways of getting information about places to go or what's going on, because local radio stations weren't that helpful. You won't find these places in the local paper or the city magazines. That's where social media came in. I had to find stuff that could tell me:

"What's really going on?

What are the cool places to hang out?

Where are the good restaurants?

What's the counternarrative of this neighborhood?"

Now, one of my favorite sources is The TRiiBE, a digital media platform dedicated to changing the narrative of Black Chicago. That's where I learned about the Kusanya coffee shop in Englewood.

I think a lot of White folks need to be more honest about their feelings. I think it's the only way to get to the other side

Now I invite my family and my friends to come hang out with me at the Silver Room Block Party on 53rd Street. It's a personal mission of mine to invite as many White folks as I can into these sorts of spaces. Being able to share about my personal journey is important to me.

I think a lot of White folks need to be more honest about their feelings. I think it's the only way to get to the other side.

DEAR GRANDMA –
JEFF'S STORY

MANY YEARS AGO, I MADE A HABIT OF SENDING MY GRANDMA postcards. She loved receiving updates about my family and my life. Two years ago, I also made a habit of dealing with my unconscious racism.

Then George Floyd was murdered on May 25, 2020. So in June of 2020, I sent my grandma a postcard. And instead of sharing a family milestone, I shared a milestone of awareness. I could no longer deny the problem we shared:

Dear Grandma,

Many of my friends and coworkers are struggling to stay in communication with their families. We feel a duty to discuss racism, the politics of policing, and each White person's place as a beneficiary of this system. I think of our family, of you, and how hard it is to ask you to face your own racism. But here we are. I want this to be the time that White people finally realize that this is our job.

Love,

Jeff

I think having a job that took me to the South and West Sides helped to strip away one layer of racism, like removing one layer of insulation. I think removing that first layer helped me see that we don't need armor to protect us from something we should be exposed to, which is called America.

The main work of my multi-year anti-racism project so far is shutting up and listening.

And I'm a talker. I'm comfortable being the expert on the FAFSA [Financial Aid application for college]. And I can tell you about it. And if you didn't understand the way I explained the FAFSA the first time, I can tell you about it a second way. This ability to clarify and explain stuff is a really good thing for my job. But in the world of anti-racism, my primary job is to shut up and listen to the Black people in the room or the women in the room or the marginalized people who have a translator, or the people who couldn't make it into the room because the door isn't wide enough for their wheelchair.

I tell myself, "you better listen to *them*."

The main work of my multi-year anti-racism project so far is shutting up and listening

Sometimes I literally have to cover my mouth or bite my tongue to stop myself from talking. But I think American racism is super powerful because the words don't even have to be said. I wouldn't have done this interview when I first moved to Chicago. I didn't even think about the word "racism" when I looked for a place to live. I would have been like,

"That's not racist to want to live in a safe, or safer, neighborhood."

And I needed adventure style safety. I know that sounds stupid. But I'm just saying, when you go out drinking and you're coming home at 2 a.m. you don't want to get mugged. That's what safety is for your average 23-year-old. Safety isn't involved in empathy.

I didn't think about safety as in we would want less harm in the world or anything like that. I just thought of safety for me and my friends.

So when I moved here, I looked at some magazine, like a "Best Neighborhoods for New People Moving to Chicago" issue, where they just mention all the neighborhoods on the North Side. And Hyde Park. So they have always had one South Side neighborhood in the "best neighborhood" list.

Then, I saw big red dots over Austin and Englewood on some internet site. Any person who is searching for a place to buy or live in Chicago is going to see big, red, "hot spots" over Englewood, or near Austin. I didn't see the words, "Don't Go," but I knew. Don't go to Englewood. Don't go to Austin. That's the code. Those red spots mean Don't Go. And, you know, I didn't see it as a race thing, I saw it as a safety thing. I thought, "it's a data thing. Those red spots that mean high crime rates." And then you notice "oh, that's where all the Black people live," so it's a race thing too. Definitely a race thing.

When I told my coworker that I was moving to Chicago, she said,

"Well, don't go to the South Side. If you drive the wrong way down a one-way street on the South Side, people try to crash into you just for the insurance money."

But I really tried not to be racist. I thought I found a non-racist way to reassure White parents worried about sending their kid to Columbia College in the South loop.

I would say something like,

"Well. Columbia is a walking campus in the middle of downtown. Kids can walk to various places in our very safe neighborhood. The parts of Chicago that are not really safe are not within walking distance."

If you would have called me out on this, I would have said,

"No, that's actually a really anti-racist way to not bad-mouth the South or West Side by saying 'it's so dangerous there'." All I did was add distance. And I was actively proud of that clever way of NOT saying Don't Go. I was not actively adding racist content to the world and that felt like enough. (I was only passively adding racist content to the world.)

Now I see the racism in myself and in White people in general. And that's ok. We can fight it. We can admit it. It's not a heart-stopper.

> And I was actively proud of that clever way of NOT saying Don't Go. I was not actively adding racist content to the world and that felt like enough

Many colleges, including mine, have tried really hard to stop being racist institutions. I've learned a lot of what I know from our DEI [diversity, equity, and inclusion] programs. But it's really, really hard. Because you can't land the airplane to fix it. You have to be in the airplane flying around these racist systems while you fix the airplane. You can't land outside of institutional racism.

If we could land in some kind of racist-free zone, or even if we could stop and get grounded for a minute, we could take the wings off and rebuild the plane. But colleges have to pay the bills and keep functioning within the parameters of an institution run by broken humans who are busy fighting (or ignoring) the racist ideas in themselves.

Essentially, we have to fix this shit while we're flying through it.

When I came back from working as a university rep at a high school college fair on the far South Side, my colleague said,

"Where did you park your car when you were at that shitty school? Your car's gonna get robbed while you're there. So what happened?"

I said,

"Well, when you're the college rep at Harper High School, the student reps meet you by your car. They carry your little college fair box with snacks and memorabilia and walk you into the school. So I parked my car where they told me to, and they walked me to my college fair table and carried my stuff for me and gave me tea. That's what happened. Oh, and I talked to kids about college. And then you know what I did?

I went back to my car, and I drove home, and nothing happened is what happened on the South Side."

Once you've been to these places, you notice the news about the kids. Like, every story is about some kids not graduating because they died while they were in school, or they were killed one or two years after graduating, or they dropped out and never graduated and then committed some crime. But when you've been there, you know there's more to it. It's not so abstract when you've been there.

I just think it's really easy for a White person being told not to go to the South Side to be thinking of The South Side monolith thing. Like I remember thinking about the North Side as not just one thing, but more on a granular, street-by-street basis. So we don't even need to think about how a situation became danger-ous, or *why* the South Side is off limits. We don't talk about it because we might sound racist. So we just make a policy of not talking about it. And if I am not saying anything or doing anything, well, then, how can I be racist?

I have a kid now and I am trying to raise him so anti-racist ideas come to him as naturally as racism came to me.

I hope we're raising a kid who will be able to navigate these questions naturally. I say naturally because I don't think that racism is actually natural. My kid is White identified, despite being mixed, and it feels like a privilege for him as a 5-year-old to understand the things I've learned from these times. I also feel like it's a privilege for me to be able to show him this other way of viewing the world.

So if you as a parent are standing at the door when racism is pushing in, you can influence the way that racism enters. You can't stop it from coming in if you live in this culture. But you can help someone see it. You can help someone understand what it means to be actively anti-racist.

My anti-racist journey is slow and sometimes I fail, but I try to remember, I just have to take one more step. I don't have to make it to the top of Mount Everest. I just have to take the next step.

CONTEXT IS EVERYTHING
– ALEYA'S STORY

IN MIDDLE SCHOOL, I GOT CALLED TO THE AUDITORIUM FOR A meeting with the principal. I noticed that all of the students in the auditorium, including me, were Black. And the principal was like,

"You all need to bring up your test scores like the rest of the school."

I felt confused. I did very well in school throughout my life. I scored advanced and proficient on every standardized test I had taken.

I never really thought about race before this, especially not race being correlated with achievement. My parents hadn't had the "you're going to be seen as a Black woman" conversation with me yet.

For the first time, I thought,

"Oh. Okay, I'm Black. And because I'm Black, I may be deemed as 'less than' going forward."

My mother is White, and my father is Black. I grew up in a predominantly Black, low-income neighborhood in Denver, Colorado. I had Black, White, Latinx, and Asian-Pacific friends. Up until that meeting in the auditorium, I had never associated my friends with race. They were just my friends. I felt very comfortable with everyone. But once I started to understand that I was viewed as being Black, my friend group began to change. I started to only have Black friends. I think this was partly because I grew up in a predominantly Black neighborhood and because I was very, very close to my cousins who were Black.

And then I went to high school. My neighborhood high school had very low achievement scores and luckily, I was able to attend an open-enrollment high school with a traditional program and an International Baccalaureate [IB] program. These programs were separated into different parts of the school. The IB students had more resources and nicer classrooms. The teachers were better too, committed to challenging their students and helping them excel. And, almost all of the students in the IB program were White.

So I had to decide. Did I want to be with the White students in the IB program? Or did I want to be with the Black kids in the traditional program?

I chose the traditional. In some of my classes, the teachers would barely answer our questions. Some teachers didn't even care if students cheated on tests. A lot of my classmates and my friends fell behind.

As a high school student, I was like, "This feels wrong, but I don't know how to talk about it or who to tell." This whole experience was hard for me. I didn't have the tools to conceptualize racism. I just saw it happen

Still, I excelled in high school. I think it's because I've always liked learning, and my family was supportive and gently pushed me to make school a priority. I was taught to work hard and succeed.

A couple of my Black friends chose the IB program, and they told me they struggled to make friends. As a high school student, I was like, "This feels wrong, but I don't know how to talk about it or who to tell." This whole experience was hard for me. I didn't have the tools to conceptualize racism. I just saw it happen.

During my first day of orientation at Colorado State University, I remember sitting in the gymnasium bleachers, watching a bunch of White students from my program pile in. I called my mom and said, "I think I have to transfer. I don't know how I'm supposed to operate in this environment."

Luckily, I was housed in one of the most diverse dorms on campus – it was a community that had mostly students of color and / or first-generation college students. I also worked in the Black Cultural Center, so I was able to create my own community and not feel so overwhelmed by how White the school was.

I fell in love with Chicago when I went on a service trip during my sophomore year. I was like, "I want to live *here*." That trip changed me. I found my passion for working on issues like homelessness, incarceration, domestic violence, and immigration. I said,

"This is exactly the work I want to do for the rest of my life. And it seems like it's happening in Chicago."

A few years later, I enrolled in graduate school in Chicago. My family and friends in Denver said stuff like,

"Oh, you're gonna live in the murder capital? It's dangerous in Chicago, why would you want to live there?"

"Make sure you don't live on the South Side. All of this gun violence is on the South Side. Just last summer, there were this many deaths, this many shootings."

On the other hand, my mom was very excited. She had visited Chicago several times. She was like, "yes, Chicago's gorgeous, move there." So the warnings were mostly from people who had never gone to Chicago. They had just read things about the city that happened to be negative.

Shortly after I arrived in Chicago, I went to this park near Chinatown with some friends. It was like 3 a.m. and someone shot at the people in the car right next to us at a stoplight. I was really scared, and I called my mom about it. And I think there was that fear of, "why would you even be going over to that side of town?"

However, because I am who I am (a mixed Black woman from a low-income neighborhood), I understand the concept of "wrong place wrong time." So I went back to that area because I wanted to be with Black people. And all the events I wanted to go to were over there.

Like I said, because of who I am, I don't generalize so much. I understand the specificity of gun violence, of not making a sweeping assumption about a place just because something bad happened there. When I started making friends on the South Side, I started to learn about all the stuff I wanted to do. And then I went to the University of Chicago's campus in Hyde Park, and it was such a beautiful area. I wanted to learn more. I started going to museums over there and things like that.

Eventually, I was invited to a group chat called "Black professionals in Chicago" by a college friend. It was huge. Like hundreds of people. That really made a difference because now I could interact with so many people and I felt like I was part of this big community who posted about "going out" events.

I started making my way in. I went to the Promontory in Hyde Park several times. I started eating at restaurants in the area and it was just such a different vibe than the places I went to in Rogers Park on the North Side. It was all good things. And on the weekends, I would try to frequent coffee shops over in that area, 'cause I love coffee shops.

So now I have an actual answer. When people ask me,
"What's it like to live in Chicago?"
I say,

"It's my favorite city. The people, food, art, music, architecture, neighborhoods, diversity, and culture all make Chicago a wonderful place to live. Of course there are areas that are more dangerous than others, but we can't paint Chicago or the entire South Side as a bad place to go.

Especially if you've never been to Chicago. Because there were two shootings on the North Side where I lived too. There's dangerous stuff in every community."

After I finished my graduate degree, my friend and I wanted to move. We both worked downtown, and we wanted a cheap place near the Blue Line. We found a great place west of Little Italy on the near West Side.

But before we signed the lease, we talked to some folks in the community. We just asked people from the neighborhood questions, like,

"Would you recommend living here? What do you think of this area for two young women? How do you feel about living here?"

And many people said, "It's a beautiful area, definitely move in."

Then we went to a bar and interacted with two men who lived there. They gloated about the neighborhood. So we were like, "Okay, this sounds great. Let's move in."

A couple of my mentees asked me about Chicago before they moved here for graduate school. I gave them the same advice I would have given my 22-year-old self,

"Just do some research on the neighborhoods in Chicago because they're all so different. Think about what kind of vibe you want. What kind of restaurants you like. What are things you love to do?

And you have to utilize social media too. You can ask a Chicago native about what it's like to live in Chicago. If you have this fear about living on the South Side of Chicago, then get connected to someone who's from the South Side of Chicago. Take the time to go beyond the mainstream media and common opinions. Talk to people who actually know the area.

When I did service work on the South Side of Chicago, I learned that there was so much beauty there. I saw some problems, but I saw the same problems in Denver. It wasn't that big of a deal to me. I was like, 'This is the same stuff that happens in every city.' So why does Chicago have this terrible reputation? Because while I was there, I never really had anything happen besides that one incident in Chinatown. Why don't the media ever talk about any of the amazing things happening in Chicago? I kind of don't understand.

I think your intention creates your search results

Honestly, I think you can find anything you're looking to find. If you want to see Chicago as a bad place to live, you'll find information that supports that view. If you're interested in understanding a community, you'll find different information. I think your intention creates your search results.

Tonika, if there was a singular message you could send out to people who want to move to Chicago, what would you say about it? With you being a native, I am curious: How do **you** draw people in and change what the media says?"

Tonika: Well, being a Chicago native, and also being from Englewood (the poster child of how horrible the South Side is), I have a lot of ways I respond to that question. But mostly at this point in my life, I just say,

"I live there. I. Live. There. Just come visit me. My family lives there. I know what you've heard but no, I live there." And then I just look at 'em, to see what their question or comment will be. Telling people that I live there kind of cuts right through it, because I think that's what people

forget. That people actually live there. Like, I don't really care about the statistics. You should just get to know the actual neighborhood. Try to do some of your day-to-day things there and see what the issues are. See what you personally bump up against.

TRAINS, ROBBERS, AND COFFEE – SOREN'S STORY

I REMEMBER THINKING,
"Oh my god, a robber is gonna jump off that train."
I was 8 years old, and I already knew that if I was in Detroit, I was in danger. I had rarely been there, and I don't think my parents ever explicitly said the city was dangerous. But I didn't have a lot of interaction with people who weren't White. And I heard local news and anecdotes that other kids picked up from their parents.

I think my views about race were still kind of childlike when I arrived at the Illinois Institute of Technology on the South Side of Chicago for my initial scholarship interviews. My mom and I walked from campus to a hotel, and no one responded when my mom said "hello" as we were walking down the street. We were from towns where people said hello to each other as they passed. So we felt like people were a little brusque. That was the only kind of scary thing I remember. I mean, I didn't die.

But then right after I started my freshman year, I frequently heard campus security and other people around me telling students not to leave the campus. Like the campus was a safe island of some kind.

At a technological place like IIT, there is a devotion to the statistically rational. Crime statistics were like the gospel of "I don't go there." Like, the numbers say:

"If I stick here on campus, buy a condo in Lakeview, and never touch this part of the city for the rest of my life, I will be better off."

But I didn't like to follow advice. Like, if you told me not to go south of 35th Street, then I was definitely (at some point) traveling south of 35th Street. I like to take pictures, and when I first got to Chicago, I thought that "ruin porn" photography was a revolutionary act; that I made things better if I was supposed to be afraid of a place, but I had the guts to go there with my camera. I was basically on a quest to explore "don't go" zones, which included where I went for my daily coffee ritual. I had been going out of my way to a coffee shop downtown by the Harold Washington Library. And one day, I thought,

"I want to find something closer, even if it means I am traveling south of the IIT island."

But I was afraid. And I am 100% comfortable with talking about that

I did a little research, and I discovered the Currency Exchange Café located 100 feet from a Green Line station in Washington Park. I told myself,

"With this short distance, even if those warnings are true, probably nothing's going to happen."

But I was afraid. And I am 100% comfortable with talking about that.

Over time, following trip after trip where nothing bad happened, my perspective started to change. I would be working on my homework or ordering a drink and I would overhear people talking about a garden they were working on or getting their kid into a good school. I remember thinking,

"Oh, they're just regular people. This is just a neighborhood."

Then I spent even more time in more casual, social spaces on the South and West Sides and eventually, I saw the process of interacting with these neighborhoods as less of a "quest" and more just a part of my everyday life.

I realized I had been living in a little bubble with people who never interacted meaningfully with most of the neighborhoods surrounding our campus. Some of my friends moved to the North Side or the suburbs before they ever went to a single neighborhood south of IIT. There could have been a world in which I never grew beyond the infantile stages of "ruin porn" and thrill-seeking. I could have lived in Wicker Park and then occasionally journeyed down to Calumet Fisheries and said,

"I'm better than all the rest of you who live in Wicker Park because I know that I can get good fish at Calumet Fisheries, and I've been to the South Side."

But if I did that without getting to know the South Side in detail, I'd still be buying into racialized shorthand. Let's face it. The terms North Side, South Side, and/or West Side are not about geography.

I was fortunate to be a contrarian who likes to break nonsense rules. I value experiences that are not filled with people just like me. My parents were open and loving. I didn't die on those first walks off-campus with my mom. I liked photography, which led me to be interested in off-limit places. And of course, I loved the coffee and the atmosphere at my favorite café in Washington Park.

When I first started leaving campus, I took my camera with me because I enjoyed photography. And I found myself taking photos of things that reflected what I expected to see. Things like vacant buildings and alleys and so on. But over time, as I learned more about the South Side and met more actual human beings and formed relationships across the South Side, the things that I photographed actually changed. I would still bring my camera out with me, but I would be taking photos of things that reflected the much broader range of experiences and environments that I came across when I was out on the South Side. And that reflected a change in how I actually viewed the neighborhoods that I was in. Even in the same neighborhood, I would be taking photos of different subject matter than I was five years before.

But many people don't have these experiences. And they don't learn the facts from someone they trust. No one they care about is saying, "That thing you heard doesn't actually match reality, and here's why:" So if I say it to someone who doesn't know me or see me as trustworthy, it's like shouting into the void.

You can't capture whole swaths of the city with two words

I think that it comes down to personal relationships. Like, one person says, "It's dangerous down here." And then the next person repeats that. And nobody in this chain of collective ignorance has ever seen the corner of 47th and King, 79th and Jefferey, Altgeld Gardens, or Beverly. And all of these places are significantly different from each other. You can't capture whole swaths of the city with two words. All places come with a range of complexities and people who have competing priorities, and statistical summaries of race and class and density and crime are no replacement for really getting to know a neighborhood.

I live in a wonderful place now on the South Side. It's just a neighborhood in Chicago, filled with regular people. I value the things that I like about my neighborhood, and I work to change the things that I don't like. But if I had listened to what I was told when I first moved to Chicago, I would probably never have even seen this neighborhood that I care so much about today.

FULFILLING PROPHECIES – DANICA'S STORY

EVERYONE, I DON'T CARE WHO YOU ARE, EVERY HUMAN HAS A set of implicit biases. We're influenced by our childhood, the news, our surrounding environments, and the people we spend time with. So when the conversation comes around to "where do you live?" And I say,

"I live in Lawndale," they say,

"Really? Lawndale?"

I get tired of having to explain to people that there are plenty of well-rounded families from my neighborhood. Yes, I saw some violence, but my mom and my stepfather have been married for 30 years. My family is close. Family is family no matter where you're from.

Then sometimes, people ask,

"Have you ever seen someone get shot?"

Tonika: Why do they love to ask that? I just never could figure that out. I literally used to joke with my friend and be like, I should just tell people, "I'm from Englewood, so I've been shot." Just to see what they say.

Or maybe I should start saying, "I'm from Austin. So of course, I saw someone shot. I shot them."

Tonika: That's so great. I am gonna say that next time, I swear.

85

I didn't grow up poor. I am not the first person in my family to graduate college. I attended a diverse college prep elementary school on the North Side. We had an actual lunchroom. I played the clarinet there. I had Black friends and White friends. Then, the school district superintendent decided to end the bus service to my house, and I was transferred to our local all-Black neighborhood school. None of the teachers at this school were Black. And none of them were from my neighborhood. I was 10 years old.

It was like night and day. I went from a bus ride to the North Side to a walk past vacant houses,

trash on the ground,

and no businesses.

The school had no bands. We had no instruments. There was no actual lunchroom. We ate in the classrooms. There were huge holes in the walls. I was like,

"My friends grew up here?" and,

"What *is* this?"

In wintertime, there was barely any heat. You can't really verbalize this when you're 10. But I remember the feeling. I was shell-shocked. It was like I got dropped in Beirut.

Since I came from a school where I got to use fairly new textbooks, I was tested right away and got placed in the gifted program. All of us gifted kids stayed in the same classroom for two years. We got to go on special field trips. And our books were better than the 'regular' classroom books. Our teacher actually had us doing projects.

I had other advantages too. My family has owned a two-flat in Austin for more than 50 years. Several generations of us grew up on the same block. I loved to read. My mother had a good job. She was never on food stamps. She took me to museums. My aunts and uncles had good jobs too. I had friends in the neighborhood who were on food stamps, but I was just a little buffered from the socio-economic conditions of my neighborhood.

Until recently, my biological dad was addicted to heroin most of my life. He'd been in and out of jail most of my life. When I was 5 years old, my mom married my stepfather. I had a room in their place, but I chose to live mostly with my grandparents, who had raised me. I wanted to live in our family building on the same block in Austin as all my friends. When I was 11, my grandfather passed, and I didn't want to leave my grandmother alone. So for as long as I can remember, I have always had two homes.

When I was a toddler, my cousin graduated from college. She really helped me expand my worldview. When she eventually bought a condo on the North Side, I visited her frequently. Then I would go back to the family home on the West Side. That's when the differences in these neighborhoods became really pronounced in my mind.

When I went to college at the University of Illinois in Urbana, I experienced blatant racism for the first time.

I stayed away from sporting events because the school mascot wore a satirical Native American Chief costume and did mock rain dances at half-time. The city cops would stop me and my boyfriend all the time, and we always had to explain that we went to college there.

Once a professor tried to lower my grade because my White classmate didn't do her portion of our group project. I called my mom, and she called the professor to ask,

"If my daughter was White, and the student who didn't do the work was Black, would you lower my daughter's grade?"

The professor had no good answer.

I minored in African American Studies, so I actively chose to study parts of my history that were not readily available. We had an African American Studies program that we called the Black House, because that was where the Black kids congregated. I saw members of the Black Panthers, Angela Davis, and Chuck D speak at the lectures there. These positive experiences were impactful too.

Then I went to the University of Chicago for my Master's degree in social work. During my orientation for our first-year clinical internship, the professor said,

"You may want to stay away from Cottage Grove and King Drive. Just stay on campus."

I raised my hand and when he called on me, I said,

"Why? Why shouldn't we go to Cottage Grove? Why should we stay away from King Drive?"

The professor said something about crime, and I said,

"You know the young lady sitting next to me would be safer than I would be on Cottage Grove. Because if anything happens to a White person, the entire police department is coming."

They were a little taken aback by this. But I was like, "no offense to you, that's just how it is."

I mean, we have Mormons riding bikes through our neighborhood all the time. Dressed up in black pants, white shirts, and ties. And they're fine. Yes, there's crime. But crime happens everywhere.

> "You know the young lady sitting next to me would be safer than I would be on Cottage Grove. Because if anything happens to a White person, the entire police department is coming."

Just think about the bias being set up for these people who were there to learn how to serve underserved populations. Those warnings are going to create a self-fulfilling prophecy. Like, they're teaching people not to attribute a crime or an outburst to mental illness or some kind of trouble at home, but to the fact that the person lives near Cottage Grove and 69th.

I don't know if many of my classmates were turned around by their actual experiences in these neighborhoods. I think that kind of thing is mostly internal.

So I always wondered, "How does it make sense that White people from the suburbs are the ones who will be setting funding priorities and creating grant programs for Black and Brown communities?"

But I do remember one example. I went with another Black student to do social work at the County jail. I wasn't scared. Maybe because even though I'd never visited him there, my daddy had been in and out of jail for my entire life. But the Black girl with me had a transformative experience. She was very surprised to learn that a lot of people in jail are just normal people. They are there because of challenging economic, familial, and/or social issues, not because they're terrible criminals.

When I realized that most of the students in my graduate program were White women from the suburbs, I started to take a closer look at these systemic issues. These women would have no experience with underserved populations other than a one-year mandatory internship.

So I always wondered,

"How does it make sense that White people from the suburbs are the ones who will be setting funding priorities and creating grant programs for Black and Brown communities?"

I found myself defending adults and children from neighborhoods like mine. I would question why a crack addict from the South Side was seen as making a bad personal choice, but a member of Alcoholics Anonymous from the suburbs was seen as suffering from a terrible disease. I also noticed how the students in my program would attribute adult personalities to young Black people. Like,

they felt threatened when a 13-year-old boy was acting like a 13-year-old boy.

At 12, I was five and a half feet tall and weighed about 160 pounds. In middle school, substitute teachers would mistake me for a teacher. My son is big too – he was six feet tall at the age of 12. So I have to make this argument constantly. I think teachers, cops, and social workers are reading studies about this, but even still, their unconscious biases prevent them from treating these kids like kids.

I wanted to close with one last memory. I think it really exemplifies the lasting harm of Don't Go messages.

When I was in high school, I was warned not to walk through Central Park. This wasn't unreasonable. Kids were getting mugged. The muggers would steal your gym shoes and stuff. So we learned to stay away, especially to stay away from the intersection of Madison and Pulaski.

To this day, I won't go on Madison and Pulaski. There is nothing wrong with that area now. But from all the way back in high school, that message is ingrained. I have this bias now, like "Uh-uh, not me. I am not going over there." So more than a decade after being warned, I still don't go there.

REFLECTIONS ON
STORIES OF FEAR

So, why do people *give* "Don't Go" advice?

1. Because they are afraid you will be hurt.
2. Because they want to protect you from your misguided desire to go to a disinvested neighborhood.
3. Because someone once told them "Don't Go" because it's not safe.

Why do people *follow* "Don't Go" advice?

1. Because they are afraid they will be hurt.
2. Because they want to protect the people who told them "Don't Go."
3. Because they don't have the time or inclination to overcome their fears and go there.
4. Because they don't know anyone or have a connection with anyone from the "Don't Go" zone.

In other words, fear stops people from connecting with people and places and so fear helps perpetuate the cycle of segregation.

When people say, "Don't Go," they are often repeating the words of someone they trusted (which includes social and professional media sources). On rare occasions, the advice originates from an actual lived experience that has been passed down. Rarer still the advice is given by someone who personally experienced fear in a disinvested neighborhood. "Don't Go" is a generational problem – often people say "Don't Go" because their parents or grandparents said it to them. And so often, those parents and grandparents said "Don't Go" because someone told them the same. In short, lots of people say "Don't Go" because someone else said "Don't Go."

Fun Fact: Most people who say Don't Go have never gone.

That's one of the many reasons we wrote this book.

Like most of us, the storytellers in this book were told in no uncertain terms – DON'T GO – but, unlike most, they *did* go.

In this section, we're focusing on Fear to show the many manifestations of this powerful force at the core of "Don't Go."

- We witnessed Adrianne grappling with her own fear based on her grandmother's stern admonition to go nowhere but grandma's house on the South Side.
- And we saw a five-year-old Soren who was afraid of robbers jumping off a train as he and his family traveled to Detroit.
- Many (including Jerry and Jeff and Adrianne) reflected on their fears of being embarrassed, saying the wrong thing, sounding racist or stupid, or even worse, admitting that their fear is a part of the racism that perpetuates segregation.
- We heard Danica describe the decades-long fear she had of a specific intersection on the West Side, while also elaborating on the toll that other (White) people's fears have on Black and Brown people and communities.
- And Aleya showed us powerful antidotes to a fear that could reasonably come from an actual experience with violence: experience and thoughtful attitude.

Danica, Aleya, and Soren

Danica's story, like others we will read, points to the consequences of teachers and social workers feeling threatened – or fearful – of their Black students and clients and the neighborhoods they live in. We heard repeatedly from our storytellers, including Danica, about how it's common knowledge among Black people and some of our White storytellers have come to realize – that White people are safer in Black neighborhoods than Black people are. Something that will no doubt come as a surprise to many readers.

But what was striking about Danica's story is her telling of how she and her classmates were conditioned to be fearful of a particular intersection (near their school). And it was based on repeated instances of people having things stolen or being mugged there. In other words, a stark contrast to the foundation of many White people's fears of Black neighborhoods. They often speak of an exaggerated sense of fear and violence in any neighborhoods that are Black (and the stories in the rest of this book will be full of more of them). As you read about our White storytellers, keep track of how few of their fears are based on actual lived experiences. Instead, it's stereotypes about large swaths of, in the case of Chicago, the South and West Sides. But Danica's experience with "Don't Go" from her childhood applied to a very specific area and flowed from lived experiences of her classmates. Both ways lead to a desire to avoid a place, but their source is very different. And the consequences are dramatically distinct from the blanket statements Danica heard in her social work classes.

One of the things Danica really wanted to share with us, when we followed up with her a few years after our original conversation, was a personal success story: "It took 40 years of unlearning but I'm fine with going on Madison now."

Sometimes bad things happen in disinvested neighborhoods. In her first few ventures outside of her North Side neighborhood,

Aleya witnessed someone in a car next to her shoot at another car. We could imagine one version of someone telling this story and concluding with, "And so that's why I never go there." But that's not how Aleya reacted. Instead of being deterred, Aleya had a pragmatic, "wrong place/wrong time," "this was an isolated incident" response. Subsequent experiences exploring the South Side, and a thoughtful attitude toward the incident – both antidotes to fear – allowed her to explore her adopted city to its fullest.

But perhaps one of the most powerful antidotes to the impact of fear is expressed by Soren, who said about one of the first times he went where he'd been told not to go: "But I was afraid. And I am 100% comfortable with talking about that." This captures so much of what is challenging about race in America: Yes, we are afraid. And no, we are NOT comfortable admitting that. But if we admit it, we can talk about it, and if we can talk about it, we can find another way forward (see the Taking a Step to Take One More section).

Jerry and Aleya

Tonika: Jerry's story about his imagined catastrophe as he boarded a bus to Englewood on the South Side made both Maria and me laugh out loud. A lot. But his description of how afraid he was – not just for his life (there was that, of course) but also of being afraid of doing the wrong thing. Taking up too much space. Being a "rude White dude." It made me think of another project of mine, called "Belonging," where I talked to Black and Brown teenagers about being in locations where they feel like they don't belong. Jerry was describing the same thought process they go through when they travel to predominantly White neighborhoods. They have that same heightened sense of awareness or visibility. They say,

"I feel taller, huskier, bigger, or smaller. I'm just more aware of like, my hand movements, I'm more aware. I'm just paying attention to all of this stuff, you know, cuz I know, if I move too fast, people might get scared."

And what they do to fit in is so interesting. This one boy had grown five inches in a short time. And he said,

"You know, I used to be comfortable, I'd spread my legs out in the seat. And when I'm on the North Side train, I just, I can't. I don't do that. Like I just, I tuck myself in. I look down."

So Jerry has a window into how Black people feel. And he wouldn't have that reference point if he didn't get on that bus. I felt the same way when I was a 14-year-old girl taking the 2-hour bus ride from Englewood to Lane Tech High School on the North Side. As a little Black girl going north, I felt like, "Oh, my God, are they looking at me? What am I to them? Should I not talk loud?"

And I can't help but think about another bus story that our conversation with Aleya prompted for me. Aleya shared that she had just finished reading *All About Love*.[6] In it, author bell hooks asks,

"Who gets to be afraid?"

What a powerful question. How you even think about that question is influenced by your personal perspective. I grew up on the same block as my good friend who is male. He had to deal with more fear than me. As a Black girl and a Black woman, I just didn't and don't have to deal with as much fear as he did and does. So even though we grew up on the same block, we had totally different experiences of Englewood.

So I remember my first time as a teenage Black girl in Wrigleyville on the North Side of Chicago. After the Cubs game, I was really scared. But I could never imagine what might have happened if I decided to call the police. The fans were so loud and so drunk on the bus. I was truly scared. But I am not allowed to have that fear. Like, the drunk people would be seen as just "having fun." But my fear is not allowed on the North Side.

In our next section, we'll discover who and what carries these skewed messages about fear, neighborhoods, and people. The mundane repetition of don't go messages are like white noise causing a chain of "collective ignorance" as Soren so aptly stated. Like many of us, Soren absorbed danger warnings before he was old enough to understand the news playing in the background. But the good news is that positive messages can also go viral. As you'll see in the following stories, people can and do interrupt the cycle of segregation by becoming a messenger of a different sort – a harbinger of positive news and counternarratives. As you read this book, you may experience some discomfort – most of us just don't notice how much we are swayed by information we hardly noticed. But these messages are hidden in plain sight – once you see them, you can't unsee the prevalence. Keep reading to learn more about the messengers of place-ism and, more importantly, meet the people who stopped the flow of disinformation in its tracks.

Section 2
Messengers

LET'S GET SOMETHING ON
THE BOOKS – JOEY'S STORY

"I'VE NEVER BEEN TO ENGLEWOOD, BUT LET'S GET SOMETHING on the books."

I boarded the Western Avenue bus near my home in Humboldt Park for a bumpy ride through dense traffic all the way down to 73rd Street, feeling the heat from the weather and the warnings.

"If you're White, you'll be shot, robbed, and killed within minutes!"

But a piano needed service and my piano tech instructors had told me about the plentiful work opportunities on the South Side. As a new business owner in 2008, I needed the work. So I got off the crowded bus at 73rd Street, picked up my 40-pound bag of tools, and walked a few blocks to meet my client, Mrs. Jones. I passed empty lots, gorgeous homes, older folks relaxing on porches, and kids playing in the streets, and I felt like something was missing. What happened to the scary gangs and the rampant violence? Where were all the criminals?

To be honest, I was kind of disappointed. Because I didn't see any of that stuff – gangs or violence. I didn't feel like my life was in danger.

After I fixed the piano, I enjoyed a few pastries set out especially for me by Mrs. Jones.

Her eyes welled up as she thanked me for my "hard work."

"I didn't want to tell you this on the phone, but you were about the sixth or seventh technician I called. Because I couldn't get anyone to come over here."

I felt my 29-year-old heart skip a beat as Mrs. Jones continued. "They won't service our area, and we're not the only community that suffers."

This happened in 2008, shortly after I graduated from piano tech school in Chicago.

But the warnings started much sooner.

When I crossed Cicero Avenue and entered the official West Side, I realized the warnings were about race, not place

A few weeks after I moved from Pittsburgh to Chicago in 2006, multiple people I met in bars and clubs repeatedly told me,

"Whatever you do, just don't go south of 18th Street, and don't go west of Central Park!"

Working as a warehouse clerk/delivery driver while I attended piano tech school at night, I was struck by the racial divide when I drove the company truck west on Division Street. When I crossed Cicero Avenue and entered the official West Side, I realized the warnings were about race, not place.

The impression I got was, don't go beyond these points because there are Black people there. We showed up at the job. We did what we had to do. Nothing happened. We went back to the office. And when I told my friends later that night about my day, they asked me, So you went *there*? Why did you go *there*? and you came back *alive*?

After sharing a hug (and some tears) with Mrs. Jones, I waited with a small group of people at the bus stop on 73rd Street.

Two White police officers pulled up alongside the curb and rolled down the window and said, "Excuse me."

I bent down by the open passenger window. The officer on the passenger side said,

"If you want, we can get you out of here."

I was like,

"What do you mean?"

Then he said, "You're heading to the North Side, right? We can take you there. We can get you out of here."

Did they know something was about to go down? I started asking questions. Was my life in danger?

And I look behind me, I see people looking at me and I'm thinking to myself, I don't know what's happening right now. The officers didn't quit. They kept asking me.

"Are you sure you don't want a ride?"

I trusted the people who lived in Englewood more than the police who were tasked with keeping the neighborhood safe

Shortly after the police gave up on rescuing me and drove away, I felt embarrassed and shared a chuckle with an elderly Black man who had witnessed the exchange while we were waiting at the bus stop.

As I boarded the northbound bus, I thought about what just happened. Another day, another revelation about race and place; I trusted the people who lived in Englewood more than the police who were tasked with keeping the neighborhood safe.

I couldn't wrap my head around that day and didn't really talk about it with anyone. It was something I kept to myself for a good while. And I thought, you know, maybe someday down the road, I could use it.

When I share these experiences back home, there are several folks who dismiss them. A few will even leave the room. However, I am impressed with the amount of people who are starting to come around. Most of them are open and will listen. They don't interject. They are learning about racism.

Some people in my family like the stories I share because they see the news, and then they hear it from my perspective. I feel like sometimes I'm playing messenger, Tonika, from your community back to my White suburbia. My White suburban land.

LIVERPOOL
YOU'LL NEVER WALK

Return
to Paradise

CHICAGO

Noname
BOOK CLUB

BEAST
1,000,000 EYES

LOVE

COMMUNISM

RACIST WORMS –
EVA'S STORY

I WAS AWARE OF RACISM, BUT I DEFINITELY HADN'T EVER HEARD the term "White privilege." I think about growing up in a predominately White suburb of Chicago and watching local news and Chicago-based TV channels. The crime reporting is so heavily focused on the South Side that I feel like the fear of these neighborhoods just slowly worms its way into your brain.

I started a job in Englewood at a nonprofit at Kennedy-King College called Common Threads when I was 21 years old. I had moved to Chicago for graduate school at Loyola, and my work hours were from 9:00 a.m. till 2:00 p.m. Even though I worked there in the middle of the day, my family, my friends, and even my peers were like,

"Be careful. And don't wear anything flashy."

I wasn't too worried. Common Threads even had their own parking lot. For a while though, I have to admit I was scared to get on the CTA train, and the warnings made me second-guess my decision to take this job more than once.

But after taking the train (the Blue Line to the Green Line) to Common Threads for just one week, it felt like business as usual. Obviously, nothing was happening. It was just regular living and going to work. Also, the people in Englewood were way friendlier than the people in my North Side neighborhood. So it was kind of like, "Okay, well this part of Englewood does feel like a really friendly, inviting and nice place." I never felt unsafe. I always felt safe. After a while, the warnings started to annoy me. I wanted to say something like,

When's the last time you were there, oh person-who's-warning-me-about-this-neighborhood-you've-probably-never-even-been-in?

At that time, I lived with friends on the North Side, twenty-somethings, we had parties all the time. So naturally it would come up that I was working in Englewood. White folks almost always reacted like, "Huh? Englewood?! Do you feel safe there?"

I've heard those questions so many times. Eventually, I developed a canned response, which was something like, "Yes, I feel safe. It's fine. I'm there in the middle of the day. And people are much friendlier there than they are here. Even just on the sidewalk, people say, 'Hi, good morning'." Now I can also say I never experienced that level of friendliness on the North Side. And that's not something I experience now.

When I started graduate school at Loyola, the warnings got even worse. I lived in Logan Square for a while, and I was like, "Come on guys."

All of the messaging eventually triggered my fear. Like someone always needed to remind me

I got warnings about the West Side too. I moved in 2012, when Logan Square was becoming less affordable. All of my friends lived there, so I really wanted to be nearby. I was riding a bike a lot so I figured it would be super convenient to live in Humboldt Park; I could just shoot up California and be with my friends in Logan Square. I found this beautiful, totally affordable place in a really old building that looked right out onto the park. I was pretty stoked, but then I was talked out of moving there. My parents and my boyfriend were concerned that I would be coming home alone late at night to this place that bordered the park. So I let that apartment go and ended up moving to Old Irving Park further north.

I wasn't *naturally* afraid of living in Humboldt Park. All of the messaging eventually triggered my fear. Like someone always needed to remind me, "You're a single, White female, and you're going to be coming home late, potentially."

Let me just add, I've had my car broken into in only one neighborhood and that was Noble Square on the near West Side (the White side of the West Side). No one broke into my car when I was in Humboldt Park on the West Side or Englewood on the South Side or anywhere else.

In central Illinois, where I went to college (at Illinois State University), a lot of the students come from very low-income households in all-White rural communities. Whenever racism would come up in a classroom conversation, the response was always like, "But we're poor too. We had it really hard too."

There were some progressive conversations in Women and Gender Studies, but I learned about cultural sensitivity only on a surface level when I was a psychology student. Privilege was not discussed in any of my classes (even though you have to be aware of your privilege to be culturally sensitive). I literally never even heard the term White privilege until way later. My friends and family didn't talk about privilege. And I just felt like there was never a good way to explain it. I had to learn about White privilege from Tumblr and Twitter.

I was afraid to take that job in Englewood. Definitely. But I am the kind of person who wants to form my own opinions and make my own judgments. If someone tells me to feel a certain way, I tend to go in the opposite direction. I'm kind of resistant to just accepting someone's judgment or opinion at face value. I had already made the decision to become a social worker, and I was really excited about starting school at Loyola.

I think in a way, it almost felt like a challenge to me. I was challenging myself to just go to this neighborhood because how can I be a good social worker and write off three-fourths of the city? That's absurd. I needed to care about people no matter where they lived. I figured that lots of other social workers were going to the South and West Sides, so I would probably be fine.

How can I be a good social worker and write off three-fourths of the city? That's absurd

After I finished my Master's Degree in Social Work at Loyola, I worked as a case manager for folks on Medicaid in managed care organizations. My team was made up of social workers and nurses; my colleagues lived all over the city. So I worked with a lot of South Siders who lived in the neighborhoods where I was working. I think that helped to keep the conversation a little more even-keeled. But there were basic lessons in how to be safe. Little things I would never think of like make sure you have an escape route, don't turn your back to the door. I never really follow these rules and after seven years of doing home visits, I've never once had an issue. No matter where I was.

I've definitely heard White colleagues express hesitation to go to certain neighborhoods. Some people even cut the visits short, or don't spend as much time with the individual during their assessment. Just trying to go and get in and get out. I wonder about this. I mean, the reason you're doing a home visit in the first place is because it's so helpful to see someone face to face, to assess their immediate environment and their safety in their home environment. A lot of the folks we visit are people with disabilities or chronic illness, and lots of folks are very isolated. You can't really do this job effectively over the phone, or in a shortened time.

I also wonder how many of my White colleagues are even conscious of how their fear affects the way they treat their South Side clients. I would imagine there is an influence there, because so many of these social workers were from Michigan or Ohio, or the suburbs. So their first experience of going to the South Side was through work. I kept being honest about my experiences. And it just felt kind of ridiculous to me that there was this exaggerated fear of going south of a certain street.

I just wish local news was less hyperbolic. I don't know. It's tough. I don't know what the solution is, but I just wish people were more open. I think it really goes deep. Because there's just a lot of internalized racism that has been taught to a lot of White people, especially in the suburbs, for literally their entire lives. And so it takes conscious effort to break it. I wish I had the answer.

I think part of processing, dismantling, and getting through the racism that we are all taught by society from birth is to acknowledge how we felt in the past. To tell the truth about what we didn't know. This is what we should all be doing, you know. I'm just trying to get there.

FOLLOWING THE PACK – TOM'S STORY

I PROBABLY FOLLOWED SOMEBODY ON INSTAGRAM WHO FOL- lowed somebody who followed Tonika and Folded Map. I was like,

"Damn, this is a real conversation. Everyone's aware of this, and no one talks about it. This is a real need."

And then when you came out with the request for stories about "Don't go to the South and West Side," I was like,

"Damn, Tonika hit the nail on the head again."

I had *just* been thinking about this. I lived in the suburbs for a second, and I was like, I gotta move back to Chicago. So I was looking at living in different areas of the city and thinking about all of these warnings, not only from my childhood, but more recently too. I remember being in the car with my dad and he's like,

"Oh, you can live here, there's White people living here."

Oof. I remember so many cringeworthy comments now. So I wanted to be honest. I just wanted to share my story.

When I was a kid, we mostly went to places on the North Side. I remember the general ominous feeling as we would drive towards Comiskey Park on the South Side for a Sox game, the comments about how the neighborhood "got bad." I remember being like,

"Oh my God, where are we going?!?" As a child, I'm like,

"Okay, I gotta keep my shit together, while we're in this place." And so we'd park somewhere and just sort of rush in this little group to the park. We were probably holding hands, at least while I was young. All huddled together in a defensive little pack, rushing to safety.

I also remember this general feeling of suspicion. Like if people didn't look like a White family from the suburbs, they were suspect. We stayed away from people like that. And also, "don't talk to anybody." If a person looked like they didn't have a home or if they were just Black or Brown, the adults would be like,

"Just keep walking. Don't say anything, just keep walking!" There'd be people playing buckets on the way in, some of them pretty talented drummers. And my dad would be like,

"Don't look at them!"

I remember we were going to the Museum of Science and Industry, and we got off the interstate going west instead of east towards the museum. We ended up in some South Side neighborhood instead of the Museum Campus. We saw only Black people as we drove through the neighborhood. And someone in the car said,

"Lock your doors. Are the doors locked on the car? Avoid making eye contact!"

I remember the feeling was,

"Let's just get out of here as soon as we can. We need to find our way back to the interstate. We gotta make our way back east towards the museum."

When I was growing up, no one would ever say,

"Let's check out these really cool murals in Little Village on the West Side. Or the Pullman historic site on the South Side." That was never a thing. Now I wish I could have said,

"Why? Why don't we go somewhere interesting? I'd rather go there than visit Navy Pier over and over and over again." So it was mostly,

"We're not even gonna mention those places. We won't even consider going there. It's simply not an option. We're not gonna say it might be interesting to go there. We're just gonna act like those places and those people don't even exist."

I think people believe what's been passed down to them, like,

"Oh, the Mexicans live there so we don't go there. Or the Blacks moved in, so we don't go there anymore."

If Mexicans or Black people live there, we know it's not a good place.

A person of color lives there, it's a bad place.

Those two things go hand in hand. No way can a safe space be a place where people of color live.

We're just gonna act like those places and those people don't even exist

Most White people don't think in nuanced terms about this; we see Black, we assume danger. We see Brown, we assume danger. And that's just been the general atmosphere. Danger and poverty are located on the South and West Sides. And there's nothing for us there. I was even told that people of color don't like people like us – White people.

You know, so much of what makes me remember (and feel) these things so vividly is not being told "Don't Go" directly. Because that was sort of assumed. Of course we didn't go there. No one had to say it.

I knew not to go there because of what was said to me about people of color.

Black people live there. Therefore, we don't go there.

Brown people live there. Of course we don't go there.

People of color are here, so we must leave now.

I can remember a few times people specifically mentioned something like, don't go to these places. But it was (and is) more "Black people are like this, so don't go to anywhere where there are too many Black people." I sort of connected the dots naturally over time.

> You know, so much of what makes me remember (and feel) these things so vividly is not being told "Don't Go" directly. Because that was sort of assumed. Of course we didn't go there. No one had to say it

When my dad said, "Oh, there's a White person. You could live here," it got me thinking. People keep parroting this stuff to each other over and over. I've been told,

"Never go to Humboldt Park or to Pilsen because those areas are infested by gangs and violence."

And maybe I'm naïve, but those neighborhoods don't look infested. All I see is Mexican grandmas and stuff, just chillin'.

In fact, parts of Humboldt Park are straight up gentrified.

At a minimum, people are oversimplifying the problems of disinvested neighborhoods, and in most cases, people are just wrong. Some people in my family are terrified of Pilsen. And I'm like,

"It's fine. I'm pretty sure it's fine."

I lived a year in Little Village. I spent a couple of months in an Airbnb in Washington Park. And I'm not really scared of traveling around the South Side or the West Side. From the impression I got from the people in my life, my family included, I definitely should have been mugged by now, at least once.

But I did not get mugged. I did not get shot. I did not get harassed. There wasn't even anything unpleasant.

I'm not terrified. I mean, I know there's issues and so I'm careful like anyone would be in an urban environment. Just standard precautions, like don't go showing everybody your expensive stuff. I guess I'm not really scared to wander around and just explore.

But my dad comes from a whole different time and era and mindset. At one point he said, "Oh don't go there, but these other places are good." And I remember saying,

"Do you know that? Do you know that for sure? I get it, you're from the city. But also that was 40 years ago. When was the last time you actually lived there? And the city has changed a million times over since then."

But my dad is convinced he still knows exactly what's what in all the neighborhoods. So I remember thinking,

"Okay, but you're telling me I'm gonna get mugged or there's all these shootings and stuff. But did you look at actual crime statistics? Because you can find that information and look at a map or something."

And I did that. And I remember seeing that there were more muggings in River North than in so many of these neighborhoods he was warning me about.

One thing I keep coming back to is some of these people just actually have no idea. They have no idea what is actual and scientific and real. Their reactions are just emotion based. Based on fear. Because I mean, my dad was taught, or learned or whatever over the years, that Black people and Brown people are dangerous and scary and poor and all these things. And it's just hard to get over that I guess. And it really is fear. Like so much of it is not even hate so much as just,

"You really are terrified, aren't you?" It's a combination of fear and ignorance.

You know there's also some resentment mixed in there. I was taught that Black and Mexican people are lazy. And welfare cheats. And all of these super-duper basic dog whistles that the White middle class just bought into, in the 1980s and 1990s.

They just 1,000% still believe this. They say so many things like,

"Why don't they just get a job?" or "their culture is just lazy."

They talk about culture a lot. One of my theories is that this comes from back in the day when we thought genes made people of color inferior. But now no one's really saying that. So they say it differently. And of course, everyone insists that they're not racist. Like the whole colorblind thing saying,

"I'm not racist. I don't hate Black or Brown people. I don't even see color. I just don't like their cultures."

I'm genuinely curious about life in different places, different neighborhoods, different states. I'm just sort of a traveler. I wanted to spend some time on the South Side because I never had. And also in a predominantly Black neighborhood. I had never done that. And most White folks have never and probably will never do that.

I guess I am sort of an exception because I've lived and worked with people from all over the world. I lived in Miami for a time. I just loved meeting people from different cultures.

In my foreign language residence program at Northern Illinois University, I lived on a floor with people of color from different places. We only spoke the language we were learning, so I think that experience connected us in a different way. And every summer, I worked as a camp counselor in a French immersion camp for four years. The camp counselors were French, American, Canadian, Senegalese, Cameroonian, and Rwandan.

I think I just learned that people are people. I guess I'm sort of different in that way. Like I remember being thrilled to be in Little Haiti (in Miami) because I got to speak French there.

Saying every person is just a person is sort of hippie-like I guess. I don't know. I feel like the idea of people being people shouldn't be just a hippie stance.

It should be a human stance.

GLITTER –
ZACHARY'S STORY

MY PARTNER AND I CELEBRATED THE FOURTH OF JULY AND his recent graduation from the University of Chicago at The Point in Hyde Park. We were drinking and it was a beautiful day. A lot of picnicking, bonfire, sparklers, and all that. We started to see fireworks and we were like,

"Oh, we obviously need to go further south to the beach so we can go swimming and see fireworks lighting up in front of us."

I left my camera unattended on the beach while we swam in Lake Michigan. When we came in from the water, I realized my camera was stolen (which was kind of my fault I feel like). People gave me money to replace the camera because I was super broke at that point. And then my dad was like,

"You have to claim this loss on your insurance."

To make a claim, I had to file an incident report in Lakeview on the North Side where I live. At the precinct, I was like,

"Yeah, so I was at this beach. At this time. And I left my camera on the beach while we went swimming. And my camera was stolen from me." And the officer, who was White, and probably assumed I was White (though I'm half-Mexican and half-Irish) because I was in the White neighborhood of Lakeview, was like,

"What? Why were you there? You shouldn't be over there.

That area is just heaps of trash. There's nothing good for you over there."

I was confused. I was like,

"What? I had an amazing day. It was like the best day ever. It was so picturesque. I don't know what you're talking about."

But the officer just kept talking about "those people" and how "they'll steal anything." I wondered why he was saying all these things to me.

Why was he telling me I shouldn't be over there?

Why did he think he had some right to say where I could go? I just couldn't believe how many times he called that area by the beach trash. He just kept saying,

"That area is trash. I mean the whole surrounding area, there's nothing that will ever come of it. It's just heaping piles of trash." And I was like,

"It's not. There's a beautiful . . . everything about there is beautiful." And then I was like,

"Whoa, you're really telling me not to go somewhere?"

I attended high school at Brother Rice, a mostly White all-boys Catholic school on the South Side. I remember a party at a high school friend's home in Washington Heights on the far South Side. A lot of students from Brother Rice showed up. It was weird because there was such a mix between my friend and his friends who lived in Washington Heights, and friends from all these other Catholic schools plus the Chicago High School for Agricultural Sciences. I was surprised that so many people showed up. I was one of the first guests there. And I was just like,

Wow, all these White people are out here on the South Side. It was just really interesting to me. But there was underage drinking so that was also a draw.

And the next day, people were talking about it like, literally, "Oh, I didn't get shot. Wow, great party. I can't believe it. I'm so cool because I braved the frontier and went to the 'hood."

When I was a senior, there was a Black student from Brother Rice who was threatened with a noose. I remember being like,

"How are these things going unaddressed with the students? What is the culture that they're creating within this school?"

Most of my high school teachers grew up in the city, and they had long family lineages, mostly Irish. They liked to talk about times when the neighborhoods were more White. And when it was more populated with businesses and stuff. So when some Black students would say where they lived, they were met with a lot of adversity from other students.

A friend of mine was mocked all the time for living in Roseland, a majority Black community on the far South Side. I learned to be cautious about sharing where I was from, Morgan Park (a mostly Black South Side community). I wouldn't talk about it if I could avoid it. If I had to answer, I said I was from Beverly, which is right by Morgan Park and not considered a bad place to be from. That changed as I grew older: I would deliberately add "that's the South Side." I was at that point trying to advocate for not generalizing people from there. When I got to college at Loyola and met people who were not from the city, I would say, "I hate to tell you, but you are wrong about the people who grew up where I grew up. And the way you think about them hurts those people. It affects how they present themselves."

When I was little, my grandma was my babysitter. Almost every morning, my parents and I drove from our house to my grandma's house in Brighton Park (a mostly Latino community on the Southwest Side).

Brighton Park was considered worse than Morgan Park, but Morgan Park wasn't great to be from either.

You know, growing up with my grandma in Brighton Park, I just felt like a kid who loved being at his grandma's house. But I didn't always feel like I had freedom of movement. You know, I would go to the corner store. And I would buy candy. And then one day, it was,

"Oh, a little boy got shot there. You can't go there anymore." And I was like,

"Okay, I'll stay in the house now." I didn't think of it like a big deal or anything.

I was told for a long time by educators or even at times my own family,

"No, don't go there. You don't want to end up over there." Just like offhand,

"Oh, no, we don't go there," or

"There's nothing for you to do over there."

> That might be the most important part. When you forget that people – real people – live in these places. And that they do the same thing that everyone else does

And then back in Morgan Park, I would walk along Western with my friends, and we'd pick up all the trash on the curbs. Because I noticed how the trash got worse as we drove home from my grandma's. I was 7 or 8 years old, trying to clean up my neighborhood. I remember we called litter "glitter."

The (g)litter, calling places trash, and all of the other warnings people toss out about places like where I grew up, hurts the places because it deters other people from going there, and from spending their money there. And hurts the people who live there who are dehumanized because these warnings and stuff deter us from seeing that real people actually live in these communities.

That might be the most important part. When you forget that people – real people – live in these places. And that they do the same thing that everyone else does – which is, you know, eat, sleep, go to work, whatever. People have a hard time humanizing the South Side. And people from the South Side suffer when we choose to only explore North Side areas. It's something I always try to bring back to people's minds. People live here.

AT THE CENTER OF
EVERYTHING –
KATHERINE'S STORY

I WORKED FULL TIME AT CENTRAL CAMERA COMPANY, LOCATED a few blocks from Madison Street downtown. (Fun Fact: Madison Street is the "oo" line, the middle crease in the Folded Map project). I experienced a lot of stress in crafting a response to the following questions / scenarios.

I'm at the sales counter at Central Camera Company, and a tourist customer:

expresses enthusiasm about exploring Chicago, but trepidation about venturing to the South Side. Sometimes they repeat a warning they received before they visited the city. What do I say in response, and when and how do I say it? And how is this interaction affected by the fact I am a service provider, and the customer is handing me money?

OR

tells me they are going to visit the Museum of Science and Industry on the South Side. How do I decide which transportation route to recommend? Do I screen people for street smarts, then encourage them to consider a ride on the Green Line and a long, enjoyable walk through Hyde Park? Do I recommend the Metra over the Green Line to people who look like they have money and no patience? Is this behavior appropriate or inappropriate or just, like, *wildly* inappropriate?

I have never told someone not to go to the South Side. But I have had to negotiate *how not* to do that

What's my role as a citizen of Chicago, as a de facto welcomer to tourists, as a knower-of-routes?

AND

A friend who is considering a move to Chicago asks me where they should live in the city. Do I advise her to explore the North, South and West Sides? Do I consider her lifestyle? Do I think about her preferences based on where she lives now? Do I screen her for street smarts, then recommend neighborhoods?

I have never told someone not to go to the South Side. But I have had to negotiate *how not* to do that. The first two scenarios are ones where my status as a retail employee weighed heavily on my sense of what I was free to say. The question of what neighborhood do I (a White person) recommend to a friend (usually but not always a White person) thinking about moving to the city is a real firebomb of a question that tends to reveal a lot. It also intersects with how gentrification operates. "Don't go to the South Side" gets complicated when you're talking about going there to live, permanently.

When I worked at Central Camera, I met more people from the South Side and the West Side than I did as a student at the University of Chicago in Hyde Park. In fact, Central Camera is the only place I ever worked that actually served the City of Chicago in its entirety. I met people who lived in Woodlawn, and Lawndale, and Washington Heights, people from so far south that they could walk to Indiana, and farther west than I had understood Chicago really extended. I didn't know how segregated other businesses were, even ones that shared Central Camera's centralized location in the Loop, ostensibly accessible from all sides, until I was hit in the eyeballs with the reality of who was walking through the door at Central Camera.

I credit Don, the owner, with making sure that the store served *every* constituency in Chicago; while I was employed there, I made it my business to help the store continue to do so.

So people brought their world to me. Without working at Central Camera, I would have never had an authentic, natural interaction with the people from these places. And not only did I meet them, but I also got to know them. I went to see them in their neighborhoods. I met a man who had found a cache of school photos documenting the generational shift on the West Side from Jewish, White, and European to African American. When he came in to buy film, I felt like the West Side was visiting me. And I was getting to see these parts of the city through artistic work made by people who lived there and worked there. I really value that. And so when I drive through the West Side now, I think about people I know who make artwork there.

I was also hired as a contract worker for a Smithsonian Institution project that provided free photo-digitizing services to Chicagoans. Anyone from Chicago could get their family photos digitized for free during the four-week program. I did this work at the DuSable Museum of African American History and Chicago State University on the far South Side, so most of the people who brought their photos in were from the South Side. I feel like I traveled all over Chicago from this little nook on the bottom floor of the DuSable. I saw more of the South Side through the lens of a camera on a copy stand than I would have ever seen in real life.

Working on that project helped me reconnect with the South Side as an adult, no longer as a student at the University of Chicago. I had this lovely commute walking from the Green Line through Washington Park. And our team worked at Chicago State

University during the last week of my photo-digitizing job. I rode the entire route of the Red Line from Howard to 95th and then I walked over to Chicago State. At the end of the day I did the whole thing in reverse. Although people might say I was a South Sider when I lived in Hyde Park, I didn't really see the South Side writ large until I worked on this Smithsonian project. I think it's hard for anyone who works at or attends the University of Chicago to see the South Side neutrally.

I saw more of the South Side through the lens of a camera on a copy stand than I would have ever seen in real life

Geographically, Hyde Park is on the South Side. But Hyde Park is not seen as a part of *the* South Side that people mean when they say, "Don't go to the South Side." When people say, "Don't go to the South Side," they're not really talking about a geographical area. They're talking about a perceived cultural space, or, very troublingly, maybe the lack of space for a certain culture (White), or the lack of "culture" altogether.

I think that when people say, "Don't go to the West Side," they're not talking about Garfield Park Conservatory. They're saying something else.

I am a limit pusher. So pretty early on, even after I was told by other students at the University of Chicago that there were boundaries to respect, I was breaking those boundaries.

I was glad to have a reason to go to Chicago State. I went to see a coworker at his house on 121st Street. I remember driving there and thinking, this is so big. This is such a big part of the city. And it's so much farther than I thought. The far South Side feels different. The architecture is different. The lots are different.

But if Hyde Park's your starting point, you're stuck with myopia. Like, you have these glasses on that aren't letting you really see. And so I think that there needs to be a way where Hyde Park is part of the South Side, but it's not the whole story. And it doesn't exist separately from these other spaces on the South Side.

Like, people say that the "nice" or "richer" parts aren't really part of *the* South Side. And when I think about Chicago, I want to think about the South Side as a space that holds so many things together at the same time. And it's sort of extra harmful to say,

"Well, the nice part belongs to the university" like, "aaaahhh!" I was told in this layered way that the South Side you don't want to go to is *that* South Side, the one that is deprived of resources, safety, and structure. But of course that isn't a useful or helpful or practical framework in any way and it isn't even really what's going on.

Through formal channels at the University of Chicago, I was told to stay within the boundaries of Hyde Park. More detailed instructions came from friends or other students in my area of study. And I gravitated towards the art group, who modulated the don't go message into softer boundaries, with a larger "safe" area. I also got a more nuanced or mature view of the relationship between the University and the surrounding area from teachers and mentors who had lived for a long time in Hyde Park. But the message that I actually got, and I'm gonna really stumble over my words here because I haven't really distilled it, was that the South Side isn't a geographical place. *The* South Side is a cultural space defined by deprivation. And, "you, student, should not go to *that* South Side."

I also heard this message about cultural space when I was struggling to find photographers of color for the Smithsonian project. I asked a Black photographer, who responded to my panicked White person questions in a thoughtful, dignified way. They used the phrase, "Where are you culturally comfortable and where are you not?" And that's a phrase I hadn't heard before. And the interesting thing about that is it takes some elements out and repositions them. So it doesn't have to be about, "Where are you geographically right now?" Like, are you over some arbitrary line on a map? And I think it then becomes about the environment that you're in.

So we can see the South Side either as a geographic place or as a more conceptualized cultural space. Through either lens, there can be a scenario where you're not able to become familiar with the South Side because of imagined barriers. Either you're encouraged to protect yourself or other people prevent you from becoming familiar – that's the "don't go" message. And that lack of familiarity makes you tentative and cautious.

I remember visiting an art installation created by the artist Theaster Gates in a house on the South Side. I didn't see any White people as I drove from the campus to the house on the South Side. Only once I got to the house were there White people again. So I passed Black residents on the street and then joined the White people in this rarefied space. It was kind of sanctified with the imprimatur that signifies the blessing of a cultural idea. Like an artist who was an artist with a capital A has this project and is doing this thing here. And it's drawing people who don't live in the neighborhood.

I felt like I belonged in the house, but then I was standing outside my parked car and surveying the rest of the street and I thought, "OK, I've finally found it. I've found where I don't belong. That cemetery over there looks interesting, but I am way too far from home. I need to get into this car right now."

Another time I was driving on the South Side near Hyde Park and police had blocked off multiple one-way streets because there had been a shooting. I was trying to get back to campus and I got stuck in this hellacious wrong turn kind of problem where I couldn't reorient myself because of the one-way streets. I was getting farther and farther from the places I knew. I was passing by abandoned lots and I didn't know where the nearest gas station was. I was like, "I don't need to be here, but I don't know how to leave."

So now I sort of have it in the back of my mind that I always want to know where I am. And I think of the structural forces that have prevented me from knowing bigger parts of the South Side better. One of the things that those forces do is they keep me nervous when I should be wanting to explore. And I don't like that.

REFLECTIONS ON
THE MESSENGERS

Social psychologists spend time thinking about impression formation – how we form impressions and opinions about people, places, and events. The first impression about a place can activate an illusion: If we are told that a certain place is dangerous before we go there, we are likely to "see" and feel danger even if that danger is not real. Driving through the South Side, we might notice people "lurking" near a school doorway if we've been told that the neighborhood is dangerous. Conversely, a resident or a person familiar with the neighborhood instead just sees people talking while waiting to walk or drive their younger siblings or their children home after school.

To interrupt the cycle of misinformation requires that we identify the primary *carriers* of messages like Don't Go. Many of these warnings are passed along by our social network – family members, friends, coworkers, classmates, acquaintances, and even people we don't know (overhearing a casual conversation in a coffee shop or a warning from a bus driver on our way to work). Our lived experiences inform our views about different places too – we are influenced by the places we inhabit – where we go to school and work, where our children play, where we shop, and where we pray. In addition, we are heavily (and often subconsciously) influenced by media – everything from posters on a bus to television sitcoms to radio shows to movies to music, newspapers and newsletters contribute to our views. Social media is an omnipresent influence – Instagram, Facebook, X, TikTok, group texts, private chats, reddit threads – the list goes on and on.[7] And even though these messages come from a wide variety of places, they all end up in the same place – eventually Don't Go messages become ingrained in our thoughts. Essentially, misinformation turns into what we think we know about a neighborhood. Eva said it well – these messages are like worms in your brain – abundant, dangerous and everywhere – prevalent to the point of becoming a sea of disinformation. If you travel to a neighborhood immersed in this subconscious negativity, you don't really "go there" – you go to your preconceived notions of a place. Even if nothing happens, we say "thank God nothing happened." As if danger was imminent – even though there was zero evidence of danger presented during our visit.

And from the stories in this section, we see that just as segregation is baked into our city, so are these messages. And as Tom and Joey (and others) reveal, the messages are about race, even if the messengers try to avoid admitting it is. Place-ism, in a segregated city, is steeped in race-ism.

While Tom inherits misperceptions in some dramatic moments with family and friends – "lock the doors, don't make eye contact!," Joey gets his "Don't Go" messages in mundane interactions with people at the bar. Maybe casual conversations like that are forgettable, but then police officers offer Joey a ride to "safety" while he's waiting for a bus! That kind of message is not so easy to counter, especially if you don't have personal connections who can set you straight. Eva is warned while she's watching local news about Chicago as a teenager. After she graduates college and decides to accept a job opportunity in Englewood, she's cautioned again by friends, family, and peers *who have never been to the neighborhood.*

Zachary's story includes a childhood spent in Don't Go neighborhoods along with a rich cast of characters who instilled and reinforced the Don't Go message with everyday actions and mundane words: police officers, teachers, classmates, family, friends, strangers all told Zachary in many different ways – "We don't go there (unless we have to)" – an insidious way to say "Don't Go."

While people heed Don't Go warnings from reliable, unreliable, personal, and impersonal sources, the stories in our book tell us that the Go message is most effective when it comes from a reliable, personal source. Statistics prove their case to academics and policy wonks but for the average person, reports about segregation don't influence much. If research or facts changed minds, Chicago wouldn't still be one of the most segregated cities in the country. Even as experts on segregation, the authors of this book struggle with helping people get through this. It seems that a person has to trust the messenger who says "Go" and often that messenger has to base the advice on a personally lived experience – not "Go because so and so went and it was ok" but "Go because I went and it was ok." As Tonika says often, real change in this area begins with personal relationships and then extends to meaningful policy and institutional changes. That's why this book is full of personal stories – so that readers can get to "know" and trust the storytellers.

The impetus to help others unlearn the lessons passed down by Don't Go messaging is often driven by frustration so great that the person feels compelled to disrupt the cycle. Eva's annoyance with the Don't Go messages about her new job drove her to push back against the Don't Go messengers in her life with a different message of her own. In this way, Eva became a positive disruptor. So did Katherine, who heard a very different message from her central location in a camera store. As she interacted with photographs, photographers and families from all over the city, her stereotypes broke down and her view changed. Then she had to wrestle with how to be a new kind of messenger – how exactly to answer questions from tourists about where to go and how to get there? Determined not to reinforce stereotypes with her answers, Katherine became a "Go" messenger. Closer to home, Joey tells Tonika that he sees himself as a messenger, from her community to his circle of family and friends in "my White suburbia."

Tom and Tiana

Tonika: I've learned that some of the most powerful Don't Go messengers are members of our own family. As a Black person hearing Tom's story, I began to understand the cultural expectations and the pressure put on young White boys and girls. So now I know how much of a challenge it is to combat some of these things because it's literally, it's his family, his childhood.

And when I think of Tom's story of how his family communicated these messages, I can't help but think that we're learning about all of this together. He's learning how those kinds of conversations impacted his thought process, and then how those thoughts might affect people who live in neighborhoods like mine. As for me, I'm learning how these "mundane" warnings impact the young White people who are told these things about us and our neighborhoods. I want to know more about how he processed this, what feels uncomfortable about the statements, and when and where he heeded or disregarded those warnings. More importantly, I want to learn what he did to challenge these ideas.

For me, this is a really personal, emotional aspect of this project. I think people are learning how emotionally insidious this is; I mean, how can you go against what your parents say? And I think the only way that we can really solve and talk about these issues is knowing how it affects all the people involved. And I felt like for me, this all started by asking the question, "have you been told to not go to the South and West Side, and what happened?" Those answers were information I had never heard before.

Maria: Agreed. Family messengers are so important. But there's a lot of non-family messengers as well. And, it's not just a life-time of experiences of being told about the places in one's own city; you can be brand new to the city, and the messages you get from people you barely know can shape the map you construct of where to live or not live; or go or don't go. A side note: people new to the city are rarely blank slates – they bring perceptions from the media (TV, movies) or "just what they know about cities in America" and the messengers can be near and far – even as far away as China! But I'm getting ahead of myself – we'll get there in a later story.

The messengers start to hit us up immediately when we move to a new city. And what's striking is how fleeting, mundane, yet impactful, they can be, as Tiana (whose full story is in the From Hurt to Healing section) shared with us. Tiana (an engineer who was raised in Englewood) was visiting with a new colleague's wife at a social event (the husband was nearby but not part of the conversation). The wife was reporting what advice they had been given about where to live: "People have been suggesting Lincoln Park and the Gold Coast." I nodded knowingly as Tiana told me this. But then Tiana told me what she did next, and I was both (pleasantly) surprised and reminded of the potential power of a single messenger offering an alternative message. Tiana suggested to the wife: "You should look at Beverly and the Morgan Park area." (Side note: Beverly and Morgan Park are on the South Side; and the company they all worked for was also located south of the city so her ideas made a lot more sense, geographically speak-ing.) When the wife leaned over to tell her husband about Tiana's suggestions, his response was: "Yeah, they told me to stay away from the South Side." We don't know where they ended up living, but the story shows us how fleeting, mundane, and stereotype-reinforcing the messages can be.

In the stories in this section, "naïve" comes up a lot. Many of our storytellers (here and in other sections) are accused – especially by family and friends – of being naïve when they go (or want to go) where they aren't supposed to go. Calling them naïve is supposed to shut the person down. Get them to understand that the messenger – who is not naïve – is right. Don't Go there. So when Tom accused himself of maybe being naïve when he was challenging people's stereotypes about Humboldt Park or Pilsen, we turned this around: Tom, when someone accuses you of being naïve, replace it with courageous. But not as in "I'm courageous because I'm going to these neighborhoods." But as in "I'm courageous because I'm choosing not to believe you anymore. I'm choosing to stop repeating the stuff you told me when I was growing up. I'm going to these neighborhoods to meet people and see new things so I can stop the cycle, even if it means I have to totally reject everything you taught me about people of color."

The Complexity of Black Messengers

One of the ironies is that sometimes the messengers are Black people living in the neighborhoods that are the target of the Don't Go advice. When Roberto (who we'll meet in the From Hurt to Healing section) first went to a neighborhood on the South Side (in search of a book at the library), he was subjected to lots of questions on the train platform from people who lived in the area. Not hostility. Just concerned questions: "What are you doing here? Are you sure you're in the right place? Are you okay?"

He's pointing to the fact that the messengers are also the residents. Black people who say, "Are you okay? We know you don't belong here." So the situation is complicated. On the one hand, you're protected because of your Whiteness, and, on the other hand, we care about you. In no other kind of neighborhood are you going to experience somebody saying to a stranger, "Are you lost? Are you okay?"

Maria: That happened several years ago to my parents. They took a wrong turn off the interstate once and ended up on the West Side of Chicago in a Black neighborhood. A woman who lived there called them over and said,

"You must be lost. You don't want to be here."

She pointed them in the right direction and my parents thought the "lady was nice," but they interpreted this event as proof of imminent danger. "Even the people living there think we shouldn't be there. It must be so terrible if they would go out of their way and tell total strangers not to be there."

But as I said to my mom, "No, it must be a nice place. Somebody was nice enough to talk to you."

I think experiences like the one my parents had gives White people ammunition, pun intended. They can say, "It must be a bad place if even the people who live there say so."

Tonika: That's right ... the irony is that because of segregation and because everything is so potent and severe, the people who are most afraid are actually protected. Because we know that they're an outsider. And if anything were to happen to them, the wrath of the law would just come down. So it's a weird protection as a result.

Section 3
Shortcuts

WHAT AM I SUPPOSED TO SAY? – JENNY'S STORY

Maria: AT OUR KIDS' SWIM PRACTICE, THE DAY AFTER SHE attended my book signing party for *Cycle of Segregation*, a friend and fellow "swim parent" (our kids were both competitive swimmers) asked me a question:

"My new-to-the-area coworker asked me this morning for advice about where to live in Chicago. Although I am a lifelong Chicagoan, I just looked at the woman and froze as she went on. I was thinking about your talk last night about your book. And I didn't know what to say. I was thinking of all the points you made about how we know about neighborhoods. And I realized I was a part of her social network, and I was about to tell her where the good and the bad places were. What was I supposed to say?"

I was so glad that my book had made her stop and think about the significance of both the question being asked and the answer she was going to give. But then it was my turn to freeze.

I thought, Hmmmm . . . I don't have a very good answer for my friend. What is she supposed to say?

I'm happy to tell you I found quite a few answers in Jenny's story, and in most of the other stories in this book. I think these answers are hard to find because we so rarely ask, "I know I shouldn't say don't go, so should I just say, 'go'?"

Jenny's story teaches us that it's not that simple.

My friend from the Netherlands asked me, "What's the good part of Chicago and what's the bad part?" She just wanted to know because she had no idea. And I found myself struggling to answer because the typical answers are like,

"Oh, well, you know, the South Side and the West Side, they're bad. And the North Side is good."

But I also felt like

"Well, I've had creepy interactions in Libertyville, which is supposed to be this wonderful suburb."

But I was kind of stuck too. I didn't want to say,

"Oh, everything's great. Everywhere in the world is good."

So, I started using other language. One of my go-to's is to use a word like "heated." Like, that intersection has become heated. And here's why: When there were a lot of schools closing on the West Side, students were being sent to different schools, and they may have come from different groups or gangs, so there was conflict. And the city's response was a little aggressive. Police would just be waiting for the students to get out of school. And it would be like almost a mob scene. So I think there's a way to describe this without saying, "oh that's just a bad area." Like, it doesn't take that long to go into a little bit of history.

I feel like that narrows it down to a situation rather than blanketing the whole community as a solid good or a solid bad.

So you can say,

"It's something to be careful of if you're walking around at four o'clock on a school day. This is what's going on in this particular area. But three blocks away in the park, it's a beautiful day, and you wouldn't really notice it."

I think taking the time to dive a little deeper is beneficial for people. And it alleviates that fear where they're like,

"I have no idea why these people are acting this way and it's just freaking me out, so I'm going to avoid the area."

My friend responded to this advice really well. If anything, I noticed that she was a little bit more willing than me to, like, hop on the Red Line at 11 o'clock at night and work our way back up north. And I would say,

"You know, maybe let's grab an Uber. It's summer, and the train station is a little deserted." I wanted to give her general guidance on city living. I think she came from kind of a small town in the Netherlands. And if anything, she wasn't too worried about it.

And she was like, "Oh, well, maybe I'm just being naïve. I don't know the reason behind that. And it's different than where I'm from." But she said it in a way that was very like "I'm learning. I have nothing to be embarrassed about by being naïve."

When I started working on the West Side, people would say, "Oh God, that's a bad area. People are just shooting wildly across the street, you're gonna get caught up in the middle."

> "Well, I think the best response is just saying that you know there's a risk. You understand that. But you also know how to navigate the risk and the risk is worth it sometimes."

I thought,

"Of course you could get caught up in crossfire. And you can get caught up in scary stuff anywhere in a big city. But it's not likely."

Those comments get to you. They kind of made me feel a little freaked out too.

I remember talking to my friend from high school who had lived in West Africa, Europe, and Thailand. She said,

"Well, I think the best response is just saying that you know there's a risk. You understand that. But you also know how to navigate the risk and the risk is worth it sometimes."

I go to the police meetings across different neighborhoods, and there's almost always the same story. Like it's this intersection or this house. They have it narrowed down. And it's true, you could be in one part of a community with a very different feel from a part a few blocks over. So the more familiar you become with the neighborhood, the more mindful you can be of that difference.

When I moved to the city, I just stuck to Wicker Park, downtown, what I knew. But that changed pretty quickly. Because through graduate school, I was introduced to Humboldt Park. And I remember the first time going over there being a little nervous. I was on the bus feeling like,

"Oh, gosh, I'm the only White person on this bus. Is that bad?"

But that very quickly diminished because I was being embraced by a group of people who really cared about their community. And I learned about the history of that community.

Once I was familiar with Humboldt Park, I was comfortable there, but if I would go further towards Austin on the West Side, that fear would come back. And then I would get to know the neighborhood in Austin. And my fear would go away. And then I started working in North Lawndale. So I would go from Humboldt Park and feel very comfortable and then feel super nervous and anxious in Garfield Park. And as soon as I got into Lawndale, I'd feel like okay, "I'm home."

And if I was in an unfamiliar part of the North Side, I'd feel uncomfortable too. And then when I got to a familiar street, I would feel better. You cross the street into an area that you know a little bit better, and you all of a sudden feel the sense of

"Oh, I can sort of let out my breath and I feel a little bit more okay."

When I was a toddler, my family and I moved from Charlotte, North Carolina to Munster, Indiana. I remember it was like,

We live in Munster (which is mostly White), because it's safer and quieter than Hammond or Gary, and

Don't go to Gary,

Don't drive through Gary,

Don't cross the bridge over the river. There's public housing there and it gets a "little rough."

Even as a kid, it sat with me as strange that two areas so close to each other could be so different. It all seemed like the same space to me.

I was still in grade school when we moved to Libertyville (a predominantly White, northern suburb of Chicago). Libertyville had that bubble feeling you get in the White suburbs. We were pretty removed from the city. But as a teenager, my friends and I would take the train to Chicago and hang out downtown or go to Wrigleyville on the North Side. I think this is when I started hearing about the South Side and the West Side, like

"Those places are kind of bad. They're rough areas."

I know my parents weren't trying to scare me. They were more like, "You should be really grateful that you live up here where it's safe to walk around because you couldn't just walk around if you were on the South Side of Chicago."

I also remember my dad pointing out people being pulled over in Libertyville. If there were multiple squad cars, the person being pulled over was almost always Hispanic or Black. My dad would kind of joke, like,

"See, every time. You know a White person wouldn't be pulled over in that aggressive way." It's almost funny, comical, that every single time you see someone pulled over, it's for sure going to be a Black or Brown person. That's not right. There's something going on there. And I felt like my mom too would always bring up the injustice of having a wealthy area versus a poor area.

So I kind of created a bubble within a bubble. For the most part, my friends were a pretty laid-back, social justice-oriented group. We really liked understanding the history and I felt like it was true, that comment about, "Oh, you live in a bubble, like Libertyville's

just so sheltered." But I still think you can have a more worldly experience, even in a suburb. A lot of my friends were influential in the things that they read and how they understood the world. And my parents were liberal, they cared, but it was more about being thankful we didn't have to live there. Like you're fortunate that you don't live in this area that's bad, as opposed to really understanding the area and maybe looking at it beyond just being bad.

Then, I had a unique experience in my freshman year at the University of Illinois in Urbana. My first roommate was a friendly White girl from an affluent family in the northern suburbs. Halfway through the year, she rushed a sorority and moved out. My second roommate was a Black girl from the South Side of Chicago. She was also great. I remember her telling me she didn't really have a lot of White friends and didn't really hang out with a lot of White people. I thought it was kind of cute, because after she had her Black friends over, she said everyone had anticipated that the visit would be kind of awkward or sort of uncomfortable. But it was actually really chill and just like, a good time.

So I got both of the dynamics I grew up with in my first year at college. Both roommates were wonderful. And the differences weren't quite as drastic as what had been described to me.

After I graduated from college in 2010, I moved to Wicker Park in Chicago. I remember there was always this little background noise in my head of, especially the South Side, like

"Oh, gosh, it's so dangerous and it's like a war zone." That thought was probably from my earliest memories of hearing about Chicago.

But then again, I thought like I did in Munster. It just seemed like these spaces weren't that far apart. How could it happen so quickly, that a couple miles from this affluent area of Chicago was a total war zone, an area you were warned against? You know, you were comparing it to something that you might have envisioned being thousands of miles away. And then I think it's easy to say,

"Oh, gosh, this war-torn country and those poor people."

And that way of looking at things makes a neighborhood a very solid good or a very solid bad. It can't be both. And if the neighborhood is bad, then that means there's something wrong with the area and probably the people who are staying there.

In Chicago, I lived on the west side of Wicker Park, which is near the east side of Humboldt Park. When something *bad* happened near me, the media would say, "Oh look at all this crime, something bad is happening in *East Humboldt Park* again." And then something *good* would happen in the exact same block, and the media would be like, "Hey, here's this great new restaurant in *Wicker Park*." So the *bad* news always happened in East Humboldt Park and the *good* news always happened in Wicker Park. But those were the same place.

So the *bad* news always happened in East Humboldt Park and the *good* news always happened in Wicker Park. But those were the same place

My first job was as an intern at the Puerto Rican Cultural Center in Humboldt Park. And it was supposed to be a "bad" area, but it felt kind of scummy to call it a bad area, when everybody there was good and everything there was really positive for me.

I think it all boils down to relationships. Like when I started going on that bus to Humboldt Park, the first two times I was by myself. I was the only White person. But after I started working with the Cultural Center really closely, I started to know people on the bus. And if I got on a bus going maybe the opposite direction, I wouldn't know anyone. And that would be kind of jarring, just not knowing anybody around you. But then I started getting off in Humboldt Park and I knew the people that would hang out and be in front of their stores. Or I knew a lot of the young people because they were my students. And so you just become familiar. And then it takes away that fear.

Which is why I think we're more fearful going to new neighborhoods because you see everyone and you sort of assume, "Oh, gosh, they're all up to no good, because this is a no-good area." But you start to get to know people and it's like, they're totally normal. And this is fine. And if anything, everyone's kind of looking out for each other a little bit more than what you might see in affluent neighborhoods.

I remember when I was in college and I came home and something strange had gone on in my neighborhood. I think some guy followed a girl who lived in my building. And she was talking to the police. And neither of them said a thing to me. It struck me as strange. If something just happened, you'd think that someone would say,

"Hey, be careful, there's someone out there." Or "There's a weird thing going on down the street." And I noticed that happens a lot in more affluent areas. It's like, we almost don't want to admit that there is a problem, so we're just going to pretend you're totally safe.

But in some of the South and West Side neighborhoods, they'll come up and tell you like, "Hey, there was a few shots fired down the street. Just be careful when you're walking down there." Or, "Hey in that house, they have been charged with selling drugs from there so just be mindful if you're cutting through the alley." Stuff like that. They look out for each other a little bit more. You start to get to know people and that takes away that sense of "you shouldn't be here." You just feel welcomed. And you kind of break down those stereotypes that come with the neighborhood.

I think some of the earlier stereotypes of, "Oh Black men, there's a lot of aggression, there's a lot of anger, you have to be careful, they're usually the center of crime." A lot of that I got from the news growing up. Even today, you watch the news and it really zeroes in on people of color in the middle of crime. And there's never any explanation about the neighborhood differences or discrimination or racism or any of that.

There wasn't any one person or thing that changed my perspective. It was a series of events. You start to understand there's not just good or bad. Like in my own family, there are behaviors that could be looked at as good or bad. But then deep down, there's mental illness, there's substance use, there's a history that creates this behavior. It's not just because this person is bad. So I kind of carried that family experience to the greater world.

I was teaching in an alternative high school in Humboldt Park. It was well known that this one kid was involved in gangs. But he was a sweet, kind of cocky kid who was kind of protective of me and I got to know a lot about him and his family life. He was a kid – 14 or 15 – with red curly hair. I wouldn't have been afraid of him if I saw him walking down the street.

A couple years after leaving that school, his picture pops up in the papers as being convicted of shooting and killing someone. And that picture made him look just terrifying. And a lot older than he was. And it was a surreal moment because I never once felt unsafe with him. But when you see that picture, it paints a totally different story. So it really made me stop and think, "Is this all that different than all these other pictures that you see in the media?" I think that was the most personal thing to make me really think through the origin of the fear. And a lot of it is the news. Or it's just that idea that you see someone walking, and it's nighttime and they have their hood up, and they have dark skin, and you feel,

"Gosh, you know, I need to be extra careful." And you see someone else walking by who's dressed up and has light skin, you might feel like "Oh, well, they're just coming home from work."

Many of my students in Humboldt Park didn't have positive experiences with White people. And so we would start clicking as a class and we'd be getting along. And then my students would say things like,

"Well, White people, but not you, like just White people." And I realized I kind of did the same thing. I'd be like, you know, "That's the West Side, it's a little rough, but not Humboldt Park, like Humboldt Park is cool. People there are great, but you know, the West Side, that's, that's kind of a bad area." So it's easy to single out individual things that you know, and then feel like the rest is still bad.

People say,

"Well, there's clear statistics that say the homicide rate is this in Austin. You can't argue with that." Then I describe either the background behind it or the situational nature of a lot of those crimes.

And I say, "I'm aware of risk and I'm taking measures to not put myself at risk." You don't have to be like, "Oh no Humboldt Park isn't bad, it's good. Everything's good. It's perfect. You can walk around, do whatever." You can still be aware that it's a crowded city. There's a lot of people, there's a lot of coming and going. And so there could be dangerous situations everywhere.

People are funny. Even now I can't think of any one person or group of people that created these stereotypes. They just sort of have been emphasized in so many different ways over time. And I think a lot of well-intentioned people repeat them without really thinking about it. Like I for sure said "bad neighborhood" for a really long time and didn't mean anything by it. But then, I think it started clicking like "Well, is that making it worse to say stuff like that?" Are we enabling people to continue having this one-sided version of the community?

HARMFUL MUNDANE /
HELPFUL MUNDANE –
SARA'S STORY

BEFORE I CAME TO HYDE PARK FOR GRADUATE SCHOOL AT THE University of Chicago, people back home in Beijing kept telling me how great the university was, except for one thing,

U of C is in a terribly sketchy area – shots flying everywhere!

After I told people I was going to U of C, it seemed like everyone from Beijing to Lakeview had an opinion about where I should (not) live. They said things like,

"Hyde Park is a war zone!

To be safe, you need to live in Lakeview.

Hyde Park – and *only* Hyde Park – is an oasis on the South Side.

You can live in Hyde Park.

Don't go to Hyde Park!

Don't go *anywhere* outside of Hyde Park."

I was working at the time, and one of my coworkers was also attending University of Chicago and she said,

"Do *not* live near campus. You should live in Lakeview."

I was confused. And then she's like,

"Look, it's a really sketchy area!"

I definitely felt trepidation. I emailed the people who were renting me a home and I was like,

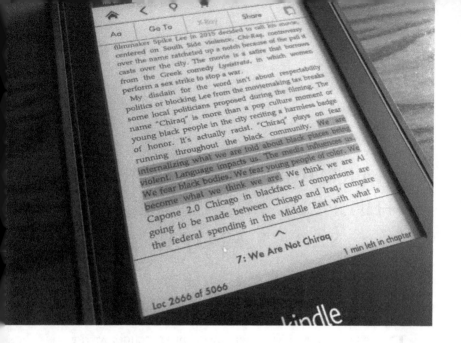

filmmaker Spike Lee in 2015 decided to call his movie, centered on South Side violence, Chi-Raq, controversy over the name ratcheted up a notch because of the pall it casts over the city. The movie is a satire that borrows from the Greek comedy Lysistrata, in which women perform a sex strike to stop a war.

My disdain for the word isn't about respectability politics or blocking Lee from the moviemaking tax breaks some local politicians proposed during the filming. The name "Chiraq" is more than a pop culture moment or young black people in the city reciting a harmless badge of honor. It's actually racist. "Chiraq" plays on fear running throughout the black community. We are internalizing what we are told about black places being violent. Language impacts us. The media influences us. We fear black bodies. We fear young people of color. We become what we think we are. We think we are Al Capone 2.0 Chicago in blackface. If comparisons are going to be made between Chicago and Iraq, compare the federal spending in the Middle East with what is

"Is it safe around there?!?"

I just didn't know.

Then I went as a prospective student to a Harris Policy School alumni reunion thingy. And the people there were like,

"Everybody lives in Hyde Park. Hyde Park is fine, *but* you can't go outside of Hyde Park."

It was whatever line they say – South of 61st and North of 49th or something.

"You can live within *this* area, but don't go outside of *these* lines! Don't go outside of this space."

So I did have a feeling – we were in a precarious DANGER Zone. Finally, I talked to the sister of a White American friend who went to U of C. And she was like,

"It's perfectly safe.

It's perfectly fine.

If it's the middle of the night you don't want to be alone walking down the street. (It's the same in any area of the city.)"

I am grateful for the book *The South Side* by Natalie Moore (shown in image above).[8] That reading requirement at U of C saved me. There's a story about taking a little girl out for ice cream that really moved me:

"A suburban friend of my ten-year-old stepdaughter spent the night at our Hyde Park home but was afraid to walk to the store with her and my husband for ice cream. She thought she was going to get shot. My stepdaughter tried to reassure her by pointing out we live two blocks away from President Obama's home and Secret Service is abundant in the neighborhood. The girl relented but ducked in and out of the store to avoid imaginary bullets." – Excerpt from *The South Side* by Natalie Moore.

That little girl was afraid. She thought she was going to get shot. That made me think. If I feel fear right now, it's probably not right. Fear is not the right response.

When I first left Beijing for undergraduate studies, I chose Notre Dame in Indiana. I really tried to blend in at Notre Dame. I dabbled with being a sorority girl. Drank in the dorms. For a long time, I felt like I was invisible. It was hard for me to be in conversations. I just thought it was me versus America. Not me versus racism. I didn't even consider that. I mean, Notre Dame in Indiana was the only America I knew. Then after I graduated from Notre Dame, I moved to California. I felt like I had a voice there. I made close friends. I wasn't invisible anymore. I think Asians are treated pretty well in California, so I felt like a normal person in society. That was so different from my time at Notre Dame. I didn't have to try so hard anymore. I started to feel comfortable with being myself.

International students who come to the University of Chicago for graduate school have no clue about what's going on. I really, truly did not understand race in America. When I came here, I was like,

"Oh, White people. Black people."

But the scope of it went way beyond what I could have imagined. I definitely thought America was post-racial. Oh sure, racism existed, but now it's gone because everybody's equal. I knew it was probably harder for people of color to do anything, but not that much harder. If you tried hard enough, you could overcome that barrier. The barrier was not so overwhelming. I didn't know racism affects every aspect of your life.

I knew Chicago would be segregated. I knew there were places where Black people lived. I knew there was a place where Chinese people lived. But I thought it was less of a top-down thing. And more of a bottom-up thing.

> I experienced segregation in a way
> that I thought was exaggerated
> before. And it just passed through
> my mind, "how could this be real?"

If you stuck with your own people, it's because you're not brave enough. Or you're not capable enough. I had no idea that so much of it was institutional. I had absolutely zero idea. I didn't know what American institutions were like because I grew up in a super-centralized authoritarian regime, a very different structure.

I thought I was confident enough. I was like, racism is not going to hold me back as long as I try hard enough.

The first time I saw segregation in a textbook way was when I moved back to Chicago from California. I experienced segregation in a way that I thought was exaggerated before. And it just passed through my mind, "how could this be real?" Just riding the Red Line, and seeing how stark it is, was kind of mind-blowing for me.

I did some volunteer stuff in South Side neighborhoods with My Block, My Hood, My City. We'd pull weeds and pick up trash and there would be people watching us, sitting on their porch, just living their lives.

Once we organized a block party for a neighborhood. It was just so normal. I think about things that might have automatically made me feel threatened because of unfamiliarity. For example, a Black man sitting on a porch, smoking weed. When I was working as a volunteer, I could clearly see – this is just a guy in front of his home smoking a joint. It's totally non-threatening. But before I spent time in the neighborhood, I would have felt anxious imagining myself being there. Instead, I had a totally visceral "this is completely normal" reaction. I realized that this scene is completely normal. Not at all scary. I don't know how to describe it. It just feels like it's ordinary life. People doing their thing. And I'm seeing it fully. Finally. I'm seeing a normal scene instead of this scary image of a Black man sitting on the corner, like what you see in the newspaper or on TV.

Another time when I was volunteering, they had a party in front of a neighborhood store after we were done working. I accidentally spilled beer on the owner of the store. I spilled a beer on his face! (I was getting tipsy). And then I was really scared. Partially it's because I'm spilling beer on an elderly Black person. I was terrified because I didn't know what was going to happen next. And in the space of that uncertainty, all those stereotypes about Black men could rear their heads. Also, I didn't know how to react. But he was *so* nice. I was able to have human-to-human interactions with people from the South Side.

I gained most of my comfort with predominantly Black neighborhoods from these mundane interactions that I had with the community. I think it was way better that way. Once I'm interacting with people from a neighborhood, I feel less and less of the spectator's perspective.

So I came to Hyde Park with the goal of debunking everyone who tried to reinforce the stereotype of the South Side. The first week I got there, people told me sensational stories of shots fired on Lake Shore Drive.

That winter, prospective Chinese students asked me if it's life-threatening to live in Hyde Park. This summer, an incoming student from home asked me multiple times during a coffee chat,

"Can I walk safely on 57th Street at 5pm???"

I defended the South Side, time and time again, each time exhausted and unsure in the end. I have a better understanding of the social cues now. When I moved to Hyde Park, I lived in a co-op with people who were very politically engaged and had lots of experiences with many of Chicago's neighborhoods. Day-to-day conversations with the other residents in my co-op helped me become familiar with more Black people and people from different communities in the city. And to understand how negative perceptions get internalized.

So I have a lot deeper understanding of what's really going on. I'm no longer a new international student who is clueless about how race works in America. I'm better equipped to defend things. When people share sensational stories about gun violence, and they're like,

"Oh, I heard like, some gunshots yesterday!"

I guess it's fine to just say that, but it's the tone that was like,

"Oh. My. God. What a shithole kind of situation."

Really judgmental. Also, recently with the Black Lives Matter protests, I hear people from China on social media just like,

"I can't believe Black people are breaking into stores!"

And I don't know how to verbalize it, but I see the way they talk about Black people. They dehumanize them, and there's no respect. Or any sort of empathy. Or any understanding of the context of Black people's experiences. And that makes me *really* mad.

I mean, segregation is the result of White supremacy! We Asians are also oppressed by White supremacy. You're reinforcing White supremacy. So like,

"What the hell is going on?!?"

I'm kind of at a loss about how to communicate this to people.

I understand where they're coming from. Because I've been there. I understand why international Chinese students would feel this way. As a new foreigner, there is a tremendous amount of fear and uncertainty, and it's extra hard for a cultural outsider to discern what is biased.

We can cite facts and figures, but people don't want a lecture about segregation

You don't know what's dangerous and what's not. It's very hard to discern without the context. I don't want to put people down either. So I just don't know.

Comments about "shitholes" reinforce segregation, but how do we explain this to people without pushing them away? We can cite facts and figures, but people don't want a lecture about segregation.

Still, I want to show how these thoughts reinforce segregation. How this idea that the South Side is so dangerous is racialized, how this idea is used to keep Black communities down. So, I try to say,

"Oh, yeah, this is a racist idea that's really popular. This idea has been around for a long time." I don't know, it's just really hard to explain all of this to another Chinese person. I need so much time to lay out the context. So the only thing I can do is say,

"It is okay here.

I've been around, I'm fine. Look at me."

Maybe that's enough. After all, I was influenced by my trusted friend making that mundane comment to reassure me about living on the South Side: "It's fine there."

Is the answer to harmful mundane comments helpful mundane comments?

Maybe.

THE CITY DOESN'T
EAT YOU ALIVE –
BECKY'S STORY

WHEN I WAS TWO YEARS OLD, WE MOVED TO LITTLE Village on the West Side in 1962 (it was all-White then). My mom was a kindergarten teacher in Altgeld Gardens on the far South Side and my dad was a civil rights activist who taught high school history. He left us for several summers when I was quite young to go march with Dr. King in the South.

In 1965, my dad invited two Black high school girls from Mississippi to live in our house for the summer. I was seven years old, and Little Village was still all White.

Shortly after the two girls moved in,

our front picture window was blown out by a cherry bomb.

The windshield of our car was broken three times that summer.

And eventually, we were kicked out by the landlord.

So, we moved into a one-bedroom apartment owned by a teacher friend of my mom's. Our future home was under construction in the new London Towne Houses Co-op on the far South Side that was designed to be racially integrated. When we moved in, there were three houses occupied by White families in our courtyard. The rest of the houses in our courtyard were occupied by Black families.

I started second grade with three Black girls from London Towne Houses at a mostly White school in Cottage Grove Heights.

By 1969 (sixth grade), I was one of only half a dozen White kids in my class. And we were the only White family who still lived in London Towne Houses.

In eighth grade, my brother and I were the only White kids in our school.

It was hard. Being the only White kids. Very isolating. It was not an easy experience for us. My brother was three years behind me, so it was even more intense for him. In six years, the color of Cottage Grove Heights changed from predominantly White to almost completely Black. Redlining is a real thing. My brother and I lived through it.

High school choice was an ongoing battle in my home. I could feed into Harlan at 95th and Michigan, where my dad had been a history teacher for a decade – I would be the only White girl in a school of 3000 kids. But my mother said no.

She registered me for the entrance exams at University of Chicago Lab School in Hyde Park. I passed, so that's where I ended up going to high school. To get there, I took the train from 103rd Street to 59th Street every school day.

The school was racially integrated, and predominantly Jewish. Many of the students were the children of University of Chicago professors. I didn't belong to any of these groups. But I became one of the theater kids in high school. That helped, but I didn't feel like a "normal" White girl until I went to college in Oklahoma. And then I still felt completely weird because I grew up in an urban, not a suburban, environment.

I feel like I turned into a split personality in grade school. I would be talking on the phone with my girlfriends and I'm listening to Motown and I'm being the girl, you know. And then I would turn around and talk to my parents like a White girl would.

Now if I start talking in the talking-to-my-Black-friends-from-school-code, my friends look at me like I'm fake or weird or like, "what the hell?" But I really do know what I'm talking about.

So when I went to college in Oklahoma in 1976, there was one view of Chicago: Al Capone and the ghetto. I was like, really? That was 60 years ago.

But people have these viewpoints, and now we all stay within our social media bubbles. And what we believe just gets reinforced instead of any different opinions. The city of Chicago has a bad national rep. So does Los Angeles. I've never been there, but I tend to have my ideas of what Beverly Hills must look like. And what Crenshaw must look like.

But I don't really know. I'm guessing.

There are probably very nice areas in Crenshaw where I can walk around. And maybe I'm wrong about that. I just don't know. And so that's what we all live with. These perceptions from outside of our actual experience. Until you have someone you trust who actually knows the area tell you differently, you just don't know any better.

I've never been there, but I tend to have my ideas of what Beverly Hills must look like. And what Crenshaw must look like

Those of us who live here know. The idea of Chicago as Al Capone, White, and the ghetto is 80% completely false. And walking around Edgewater, or Lincoln Square, or Roscoe Village, or Hyde Park, or Pill Hill, or South Shore, it's all the same. Same architecture. It's the same. And when people keep up their homes, it's a nice neighborhood. You know? It's pretty simple. So that part frustrates me. Always.

People think that the South Side and West Side are one thing. That everything is blanketed in this one view. And it's like, "No, Chicago always has been 600 little cities connected to each other." And a lot of those neighborhoods were Bohemian and Polish, and now they're Hispanic, or now they're Black, or whatever. And different groups have come through different neighborhoods, but they've always been those little cities next to each other. And you have to appreciate that there are plenty of beautiful things on the South Side.

But you know, when you're with all White people all the time, you don't even . . . it's not even part of the conversation. Because nobody sees it. And it's not in your face.

I've spent my life telling folks that their fears of the South Side are largely untrue. But I'm not the activist that my father was. So it's not like I ever get on a soapbox about it. But if somebody says something that's just plain old wrong, or ill-informed, and they're actually friends of mine, I will put them straight.

> It's not like I ever get on a soapbox about it. But if somebody says something that's just plain old wrong, or ill-informed, and they're actually friends of mine, I will put them straight

I will walk them through neighborhoods in Chicago to prove to them:

The city doesn't eat you alive.

THE BUBBLES –
HALLE'S STORY

I DIDN'T KNOW THAT I WAS SUPPOSED TO HATE BLACK PEOPLE. When I started to realize that there were groups of White people who didn't like Black people, I got genuinely confused. I was like,

"Why would you not like Black people? All it is, is just a chemical in their skin that is making their skin darker than yours."

So it just seemed odd to me. And as my life went on, I just started to kind of grapple with that idea. Why do we have to hate these people just because they have a chemical in their skin?

I think I felt this way partly because of my grandmother, who was always "it doesn't matter the color of their skin, you treat them like you would treat Jesus Christ Himself, yada, yada, yada." The golden rule was really, really big in my household. My grandmother was very much like,

"Do unto others as you would have them do unto you." Bible verses. Things like that. So my brother and I grew up to be very altruistic, and very giving to others. And then I went to a high school that was about half Black and half White. My graduating class was only 89 students, and we didn't really have any racial tensions. When we were at lunch, it was like every table was mixed Black and White, for the most part.

I mean, we had some students that were kind of the outcast type. There were little pods of poor White people, labeled "White trash." But for the most part, we mixed. Our classes were all mixed Black and White. Sports teams were all mixed Black and White. I can't think of very many situations where it was predominantly White in one part and Black in another. We kind of evenly mixed.

This is why, as I got older and I moved into different environments, I was like,

"Wait, we're supposed to hate Black people? What?"

I got to college in Ohio, and I took a class in urban studies, and the professor was talking about how when Black people move into a neighborhood, that makes White people want to move away. And I'm sitting there going,

"Huh? Why would they want to do that? That seems stupid to me."

I started to realize that my high school environment was very beneficial in the sense that it was separate from what "real life" is about. I didn't know that I was supposed to hate Black people. But I would implicitly get these ideas from people.

My parents didn't really talk about race. But they would say things every now and then that kind of unconsciously implied that maybe I shouldn't hang out with those people because they lived on the wrong side of the tracks. Like in Oberlin, Ohio, where I grew up, there's definitely a Black side and a White side and there were little things that were implanted into my brain over time like,

"You really shouldn't go over there. You shouldn't hang out with her because she lives in the projects."

And the friends that I grew up with would give me the same general idea. It was weird because I would get two competing things. It would be my grandmother saying, "everyone's equal." But then my parents kind of implicitly saying, "Don't go over there."

I think that it came from a good place. My parents definitely are not racist. Well, I mean, everybody's racist, but they're definitely not the type that are like, you shouldn't hang out with these people simply because they have dark skin. I think racism is so deep seated in White people that we don't even see it until something obvious happens. And also, it's painful to think that anyone I know is racist. That's why it's helpful to read books about this and admit that all White people are on some level racist. It's just a matter of degree.

But I didn't know any of this until after I graduated from college, got my MS in Geology and started teaching in Illinois. I heard someone talk about Muslims as "towel heads." I had never heard that term before. Another time I was talking about my favorite rap artist and a person I didn't know all that well said, "you listen to that N-word music?" It was all so normalized. That's when it really hit me that I had been living in a bubble outside of another bubble and now I was outside of both bubbles, standing in the middle of reality. It was like cognitive dissonance. Like you're taught one thing, but then you're learning another thing, and they don't work with each other. I just kind of took it all in and inside I was like, "Okay, I didn't really subscribe to the idea that I was supposed to hate Black people or stay away from Black people."

> That's when it really hit me that I had been living in a bubble outside of another bubble and now I was outside of both bubbles, standing in the middle of reality

And then my parents were scared to death when I moved to Chicago. They were like,

"Oh my god, what the hell are you thinking? It's a war-torn hellscape. Why would you want to move there?" And I'm like,

"Well, cuz I want to. I like cities. I like the electricity of a city. I like the cultural diversity of the city; I like everything about cities."

Then my parents said,

"Okay, just don't go to the South Side."

So I moved to Noble Square, just northwest of downtown. My boyfriend likes the White Sox, so he takes me to games on the South Side now and then. His mom always calls him the night before, saying stuff like,

"Oh, you be careful now, Comiskey Park is on the South Side, you gotta be careful."

And then she calls every now and then, just to check,

"Did you go to the South Side on Wednesday? Okay, so you're okay, you got back?"

I know this concern from our parents is coming from a good place, but still we're like,

"What the hell? Why would we not want to go to the South Side?"

They had never been there, so I just ignored them. I wanted to learn for myself. I like to go against the status quo

When I was hired as a temporary adjunct professor at Kennedy-King College on the South Side, all of my friends were like,

"Oh, my God, don't go to 63rd and Halstead. Don't ride the Green Line."

They had never been there, so I just ignored them. I wanted to learn for myself. I like to go against the status quo. Also I was like,

"I need the money. This advice is ridiculous."

So I took the Green Line to Kennedy-King twice a week. I had all these ideas in my head like,

"Oh, there's gangs. I'm gonna get shot."

But I loved taking the train. And the students were great. They loved to go to school, for the most part. They were easy to work with, eager to learn. I signed on to teach semester after semester. I just felt like,

"Yes, I want to do this again and yes, I want to do this again, and again."

The environment *was* different, but I never felt out of place. I never felt like I shouldn't be there. I made a lot of very good friends who are still always down for hanging out. The whole experience was great.

Eventually, I got a more permanent job at Malcolm X College on the near West Side. So the college is not on *the* West Side, or the South Side, but still I get people who are just like,

"You work at Malcolm X? Oh, my God, I feel so sorry for you." And I'm like,

"Why? Why would you feel sorry for me?"

At a meetup I did in the suburbs once, a person told me that Malcolm X College was a place where they taught Black militants to be Black Panthers. But Malcolm X wasn't a Black Panther.

So I was like,

"No, it's a regular college with regular people."

People who didn't know anything about Malcolm X or the environment of the college were genuinely scared for me. And again, I'm just looking at them funny, like,

"Why are you scared for me? I'm an adult. I'm completely capable of judging."

I think a lot about the bubble that I live in versus the bubble that these people live in. It's like in the movie, The Matrix. They don't know they're plugged into this matrix, that they live in this bubble where White people are taught to be scared of Black people.

RENT A WHITE LADY –
CAROLINE'S STORY

I GREW UP IN A PREDOMINANTLY WHITE SUBURB NORTHWEST OF Chicago. My family and I visited the officially-sanctioned-South Side places-where-White-people-can-go, like the Museum of Science and Industry. We never even thought about going anywhere else on the South Side.

Luckily, I went to Northwestern University where I had the good fortune to meet Eileen and Kenny. Like me, Eileen came from a big Irish Catholic family and neither of us were currently (or on our way to becoming) seriously rich. We graduated in 1982 with the heiress to the Caterpillar fortune, the future wife of David Letterman, and the heir to the Wexler coffee empire.

Eileen and I had to get work study jobs to make ends meet. That's how we met. Then Eileen made friends with Kenny. And that's how I met him. He was our dorm custodian. He was only 20 years old, so we were close in age, but most students didn't think of him as a possible friend. They treated him more like an anonymous worker. But not my Eileen. She invited Kenny to drink beer and eat pizza with us in her dorm room. At first, Kenny was reluctant. I could tell he was nervous, and I thought that was odd.

Now I understand that because he was a Black man and a custodian in a college dorm, Kenny was taking a big risk by socializing with us. One day, he asked us to watch him play basketball at Washington Park on the South Side, like a dare. He was like,

"You guys have no idea what it's like for me to come up to Northwestern, and just be a silent witness to everything around me. You've got to come to Washington Park and watch me play basketball. Meet me at the field house."

So we borrowed somebody's car (it's hard for me to remember how we did things without Google Maps and cell phones) and followed a street map to Washington Park. Then we drove in circles around the park trying to find the field house.

At one point, a police officer pulled us over and said,

"You are in the jaws of death here. Go home immediately."

We told him we were there to see a basketball game. And we asked him for directions to the field house. He was like,

"No, I am not giving you directions. You two do not belong there."

We asked him again. And he said,

"No, you absolutely cannot go there."

I don't really remember what happened after that, but we finally found the field house and went inside to watch the basketball game. This was probably the first time I was one of the only White people in an all-Black space. And

nobody killed me,

nobody shot me,

nobody even glared at me. Like, I don't think anybody even gave us a second look. I mean, in my mind, everybody would have been staring at us, but that's not what happened. So we returned alive (and well) after being in the "jaws of death."

I started to understand that White people are just crazy to think that Black people spend all of their time thinking about how they can kill us. It's just insane that White people walk around thinking that we are the only ones that the Black people around us are thinking about. I mean, they're going to disrupt their whole day just to mess with me? Why? There's no gain.

I live in Garfield Park and yes, bad stuff happens. I worked with my neighbors to shut down an open-air drug market near us. (This wasn't complicated. We just needed someone to install a lock on a gate.) Someone was shot and killed in front of our house. I have been held up by a young person, and someone tried to break into our house and attack me. But the way I see it, *I* am not the target of these random crimes. I don't automatically think,

"Oh I need to live somewhere safer."

I think the crimes that happen here could happen anywhere in the city.

In my neighborhood, people say hello, they stop and talk to you when you're in your front yard. I put cherries from my cherry tree out in a basket on the sidewalk and people come by and chat about the cherries. I call this, "cherry-tree diplomacy."

No one believes me when I paint a picture of my neighborhood as an ordinary place where people are just living their lives, offering neighborly greetings, digging their cars out of the snow, and hoping for a little sunshine.

Early on in my career, I was working for Columbia College, providing guidance to students at one high school on the South Side, and two on the West Side. I took public transportation past the Garfield Park Conservatory on the West Side. And nobody was ever there. I got off the train once and walked through the conservatory. It was like a ghost town. When I told my colleague about this she said,

"Are you out of your mind?

Do you have a death wish?

What are you doing?"

I kind of wanted to say,

"I was just going somewhere other than the places White people always go."

For about ten years, between school and work, I traveled the city by public transportation. I got off and on buses and trains all over the South and West Sides of Chicago. I walked in these areas to various landmarks, homes, businesses, and social gatherings. I would nod and say hello, and people would nod and say hello back. Not one bad thing ever happened to me.

But my friends and colleagues never stopped warning me. I grew tired of this, and I began to separate from certain White people. Often I was the only White person when I visited the students in high school, and over time I became a part of their extended lives. Then I was the only White person at weddings, christenings, and birthday parties. So I became quite comfortable with being the only White person in a Black space.

At one of the West Side high schools where I worked, I met a young Black woman who ended up staying in housing shelters. I would visit her to help her find a place to live or get a job or whatever the need was. And as the other young women in the shelter overheard me helping her, they would say,

"Hey, can you help me do this? I could use a White lady to help me." And so I would joke around that if I were a conceptual artist, which I'm not, I would have done a project called "Rent-A-White-Lady."

When the young woman I was helping called a landlord to request information about an apartment for rent, the landlord told her,

"Yeah, sorry, it was rented."

Right after my student hung up, I called the landlord. The young woman and I had practiced conversations like these, so we essentially said the same things to the landlord. And when I called him about the same place as my client, the landlord made an appointment for me that afternoon. He was really angry when I arrived with my student to see the apartment. He looked at her and then at me and said,

"I thought *you* were the one who was going to rent the apartment." Then I said,

"I never said that. I just asked if the apartment was available because I'd like to come see it. I can either report this discrimination to the authorities, or you can rent this apartment to my friend." That's how she finally found a home.

It's not only the White voice and/or the White skin that make a difference – it's *my expectation* that the system is going to work on my behalf

And you know, it's not only the White voice and/or the White skin that make a difference – it's *my expectation* that the system is going to work on my behalf. As a White person, I assume that the systems around me exist to support me. So when I make a call, I have a certain confidence that my issue will be resolved.

Later on in my career, I had to apply for Food Stamps on behalf of my godson who came to live with me when he was in crisis and when I was let go from a job as Deputy Commissioner for Cultural Affairs for The City of Chicago. Once again, I was the only White person in the room. I'm a Northwestern University graduate and I have worked in highly visible positions in Chicago. But there I was, sitting in a place where there's no perceived need for anyone to hurry – it's as if we think that people who apply for assistance have nothing else to do but sit there. So I sat for hours and hours and hours. And as I looked around me, I thought,

Empowered people would never stand for the way this system is set up. Surely there would be a demand for more efficiency. No one would sit for hours and hours and hours. And there'd be an appeal. Like you would be able to talk to someone and say,

"Excuse me, but this is bullshit."

But sitting in that office, I learned that you had to just take it, and this was just another eye-opener for me.

My family likes to call me "Crazy Aunt Caroline" because I have "interesting" friends and I live in "different" places. I bought a two-flat in Garfield Park with a gay couple because they were my friends and that's what we could afford. Family and other acquaintances would say,

"Caroline, why are you, a straight White lady, living with two gay women on the West Side of Chicago in a Black neighborhood?"

But I didn't intend to live with two gay women. They were just my friends. And we didn't set out to live in a predominantly Black neighborhood on the West Side. It's more like we weren't *against* living there. And if we had any thoughts about why not to live there, it was not about being afraid. It was more about gentrification. My colleague, a Black woman from the suburbs, used to joke with me and say,

"Caroline, Garfield Park is not for White people. We want to save this place for Black people."

This story gets even better because she also warned me about the West Side when we were both working at the Chicago Park District. Our department was encouraged to "adopt families" at Christmas time and fulfill their wish list for food, clothing, and gifts. When we were done shopping for the family on our list, I said,

"Oh, I'm the person who can drop off all this stuff." I was living in Logan Square and the adopted family lived in Garfield Park, so I was closer. And this colleague said,

"You can't go there. You cannot go. Like, are you kidding?"

She was a Black woman from the suburbs, so I think she had a different perspective than Black people from the South or the West Side. She was like,

"You, White lady, cannot safely deliver these Christmas goodies to this family."

By then I had already spent a lot of time at Orr High School on the West Side. So I was like,

"Actually, I think I can deliver the gifts."

Then she said,

"Well, I'm going with you, then. You can't go by yourself."

And so we went to the house together. And not *only* did we not get shot, but the family of an Orr High School student lived there. When the mom opened the door, she looked at me and said,

"Caroline, I know you, I'm Tiffany's mom. It's me, Mrs. Johnson. Oh my gosh, come in." And then my colleague was like,

"Okay . . ."

So, not only can you go into a Black neighborhood and not get shot, but you might even know people who will be extra friendly and welcome you into their home.

After that, when we were talking about me moving to Garfield Park then, my colleague changed her tune.

"Okay, Caroline, you can live in Garfield Park. I'm not gonna kick you out."

But I was still concerned. I don't want to be a gentrifying force in any neighborhood.

There are just so many well-educated people with terrible ideas about what it's like to be in Black spaces

Some of my friends called me an "urban pioneer." And I would ask them,

"Do you have any idea that 'urban pioneer' implies that (a) nobody else is here already; or (b) that I wish to have everybody around me move? Which is not the case." Or they would be implying that I was taking a big risk living in Garfield Park, or that I was gonna make a killing one day – as in, one day this is gonna be really valuable land. And I'm like,

"Well it's pretty great right now. And in fact, we bought at exactly the wrong time in the history of the market to 'make a killing'."

I have lots of stories about police, repairmen, service providers, and random people telling me to be careful, telling me I'm crazy, telling me I'm such a brave "urban pioneer." There are just so many well-educated people with terrible ideas about what it's like to be in Black spaces.

Many years after we graduated from Northwestern, Eileen and her family took their summer vacation in Chicago and stayed with me in Garfield Park. On the first day of their visit, they were walking back from the train to my house after spending a day downtown. A police officer stopped and asked if they were lost. Eileen and her husband said no, they were fine. When I got home from work, her kids went on and on about how that police officer followed the family all the way to my home.

Eileen is super pale with strawberry blonde hair. Her children are practically transparent. They are super White. Blue eyes. Freckly skin. Like paper-white looking. But they are not naïve. Eileen and her husband are public interest lawyers who often defend people on death row. They spend much of their work life in prisons with African American men who were wrongly convicted of crimes.

The next day when Eileen and her family again got off the train near my house, an officer asked Eileen if she meant to go to Oak Park. When she said no, the officer told Eileen and her family that they needed protection because they were in the *wrong* neighborhood. Eileen runs an Innocence Project and is used to questioning the authority of police so she used strong language to tell the officer to leave her and her family alone. As he took off, he said,

"It's your funeral."

During this visit, I was sending Eileen and her family to the Mexican Fine Art Museum and other really cool places. I was like, check out this great city. Go here, there, everywhere. Go all around town. But the thing they remember most about their vacation in Chicago is those encounters with the police.

People never forget. That's the thing about warnings. You always remember.

WHISTLING WHILE
YOU SEGREGATE –
JAMAINE'S STORY

Icame to Chicago for a graduate degree in Urban Planning at DePaul University. My relative, who had never been to Chicago, told me to live on the North Side. After I spent a little time in the city, I noticed that most of the Black people from other countries lived in predominantly White neighborhoods up north. My family members are descendants of slaves, but we got dropped off in Central America or the Caribbean instead of the United States. Since I am part of the non-United States diaspora, I thought I should live on the North Side too. Total strangers on Facebook told me not to live on the South Side. So did the media.

But I don't like to have CNN or Fox News tell me about a place.

So in 2018 when I moved to Chicago, I landed in Hyde Park. But it wasn't easy. First, I joined Facebook groups created for people looking for roommates. At one point, I was talking to two potential roommates. One was Indian and one was South Korean. Everything they suggested was north of River North. If they suggested anywhere on the South Side, it was the South Loop.

But I had remembered visiting Chicago years before and I had stayed in Bronzeville. I was like,

"Wow! This is nice.

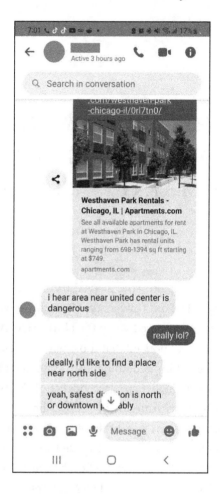

They have some really nice apartments in Bronzeville.
Nice *big* apartments. I found a great spot.
I found a three-bedroom, good price, Bronzeville.
New apartment, everything fresh, really nice, brick exposed."

Then one of them sent me a map displaying gun violence statistics. The map had red hotspots. The redder the area, according to the map, the more dangerous it was.

Geographically, this guy wasn't even checking out Hyde Park. And I was like,

"Hyde Park? Hyde Park is nicer than the neighborhoods I've lived in New York, but okay."

But he kept nudging us north.

He wouldn't say he didn't want to live around Black people. But, I mean, I was getting that vibe because it was majority Black neighborhoods. I know Black people that live in Bronzeville who say Bronzeville is fine. They say,

"I live here. I walk here. I jog. I bike here. It's fine."

Then the other potential roommate weighed in.

"I chained up my bike to a bike rack by IIT, and someone stole my bike!" (IIT is on the South Side).

I was like,

"That's an isolated event. I'm not discrediting what you went through, but I'm like, *come on, man. Really?* I know, your bike got stolen. I get it. But I mean, okay?"

I was surprised by their comments. I grew tired of trying to make the case. The hotspots on the map triggered bells in my head, set off alarms ringing.

I knew in that moment. I didn't want to move in with them. I focused my efforts on looking for my own place, because I was like, I don't want to deal with *this*.

It's kind of like a dog whistle. They showed me this map and I don't think they considered for a moment how that might impact me. They didn't consider what I would think or feel about that.

To my potential roommate, it was just a crime map. But for me it was specifically about the South Side. I explained to the guy a little bit about what the statistics are, and what kind of crime it is. We got down to a little nitty gritty. But then I just lost effort and energy and it was like,

"All right, whatever."

I just thought it was ridiculous that someone sent me a map. And I was like,

"Wow, people are very scared. They're really scared."

My almost-roommate didn't even live in the neighborhood. He never lived there. He didn't know anybody there. Probably never even visited far south Chicago. But this map is enough to push him away. And to try and push me away from the South Side as well. I just thought about these apps and these companies, these housing companies using geographic maps, to sort of, well not sort of, but *intentionally* continue to redline these Black neighborhoods, steer people away from moving there, and keep people from possibly investing money there or spending time there.

These housing companies using geographic maps, to sort of, well not sort of, but *intentionally* continue to redline these Black neighborhoods

So the map was kind of used as a way to weaponize whatever he was trying to get at, whatever point he was trying to make. I thought it was a weak argument. So I just moved on from it. I've lived in Boston and Los Angeles. I grew up in Flatbush. People would say,

"Don't go there, people are bad there! You'll get shot! you'll get *robbed!*"

I'm like,

"No, you won't. Everybody is normal. We played on the stoop. We had fun getting soaked by the fire hydrants. Our parents worked every day. We went to school, and we went to work. Sure, things happened, but it's not a war zone."

So I was suspicious when I heard the same kind of stories about Chicago.

I didn't know everything about all of the South Side neighborhoods, but I think I had just enough personal experience to hear the dog *whistle* when people sounded the alarms.

Even after I settled into my new apartment on the South Side,

I found myself still defending the neighborhood to my new class-mates and friends.

Urban planning is a very White-dominated space. A lot of my classmates at DePaul were White. So, I would get a lot of questions about living on the South Side.

I always did my best to debunk any kind of soft pitch stereotypes they threw. I didn't get a bunch of pushback, but I did notice comments here and there.

And actions – even subconscious ones – speak louder than words.

Like my friends always seemed to only want to hang out in the Loop or north of the Loop. They would say things like "the South Side's too far." And I'm like,

"What?! Then Lincoln Park is too far for me. I'm in Hyde Park, I'm not gonna travel all the way to Uptown or wherever every time you want to hang out."

But Hyde Park felt like a safe, diverse spot for my White class-mates. I think they were just more comfortable being in a racially diverse neighborhood. If I said,

"Let's go to Auburn Gresham. Or let's go chill in Back of the Yards. Or let's go to Woodlawn."

They said,

"No way."

My family emigrated from Panama in the early 1980s and I grew up thinking I am Black, but not *that* Black. I know a little something about not fitting in. I don't eat collard greens or grits. When I go to Latinx Dance Clubs in Chicago, people look at me sideways until I open my mouth. I speak fluent Spanish. I also know about how Black immigrants from different places view African Americans.

I grew up with Caribbean, Dominican, Cuban, and Panamanian people. We were Black, but we didn't mingle much with the Yankees (that's what Panamanians call African Americans). And that's because most of their own knowledge of "Yankees" was based on the stereotypes they had heard, not really because they had any direct experiences.

They heard that African Americans had a poor work ethic. They didn't get educated. That kind of thing. So they kind of steered me away from certain areas because of what *they* had been told. That's how I learned that I was Black, but not *that* Black.

My urban planning classmates were supposedly awakened in 2020. They got a jolt of energy. Let's do work now! And I'm like,

"Hey, how many times do you go to the South Side and actually go to these businesses and speak with these people? I'm not talking Uber Eats man. Let's go to Englewood, to Woodlawn. Let's go. We're planners. We can't just study these neighborhoods in the classroom."

Englewood was a common topic in urban planning discussions. I would say,

"How many of y'all been there?"

Most of them had never been there.

I could have stayed away and moved north. That would have been so easy. But now I'm glad I moved south because the South Side is awesome. I've met so many great people from the South Side. I hang out a lot over there. The people there are regular – moms, dads, kids, students. Regular grandparents too. Just regular folks.

Everything's cool. It's a regular area. Literally.

I learned so much about African American Chicagoans moving around the city. Such rich history that I didn't know about before. What have I learned about all these communities?

And I saw the people doing the work. I saw the entrepreneurial spirit. I saw the truth with my own eyes, on the ground

First, there is a mentality of entrepreneurship, and a well-organized community-building work ethic. There are so many Black-owned businesses. There are so many passionate people on the ground organizing work around all kinds of different issues.

The media never highlighted the folks doing the work. And I saw the people doing the work. I saw the entrepreneurial spirit. I saw the truth with my own eyes, on the ground.

I always share this when I go back home. I tell people to visit, say to come to the Brew Fest in Hyde Park. My barber from the West Side invited me a few years ago. He said,

"Come to the Brew Fest, you'll have fun, you'll meet people, it's a thing we do out here in Chicago."

I remember thinking the media doesn't show this. Just a group of majority Black folks coming together from all over the city and the region. This fun stuff is here. On the South Side. Organized by the community. Protected by the community. People are just out here having a great time.

That was the first time I was at an event of that magnitude with that many Black people in Chicago having a great time. And I was like,

"Wow, yeah. This is dope. This is great." And, you know, I wish this is what people would highlight.

So, come to the Brew Fest.

You'll have fun, you'll meet people, it's a thing we do out here in Chicago.

We do this every year. It's cool. It's great.

And it's all

love.

REFLECTIONS ON
SHORTCUTS

Humans aren't entirely irrational, but we are hard-wired to make choices based on assumptions rather than fact-filled spreadsheets. We are not computers. And in lots of cases, these shortcuts are harmless – for example, we grab an umbrella and assume it's going to rain without even thinking about how the meteorologist determined that rain was imminent. But when we don't think about how someone determined that a neighborhood is dangerous or "bad," we perpetuate segregation. Handed down and passed along through the generations, exaggerations and outright falsehoods become invisible informants – the kind of shortcuts that keep us apart.

It can be mystifying and a little painful to read about the lengths Sara had to go through just to make an informed choice about living on the South Side. Her story not only illustrates the global spread of "Don't Go" warnings, but also highlights the unending forces feeding into the shortcuts that help to continually cement segregation in our cities. People who had never visited the United States, much less a neighborhood in Chicago, warn Sara about the "bullets flying everywhere" on the South and West Sides. Sara tells us that her upbringing in China implanted the automatic assumption that Black neighborhoods were segregated because Black people didn't try as hard and weren't as capable as White people, but this damaging shortcut is not exclusive to China – it is also common among White people in the United States.

In tackling the labels "good" and "bad" neighborhood, something that rolls off our tongue so easily in so many contexts, Jenny's story reveals many sometimes-subtle ways that our default thinking is built up (the media labeling the same geographic space a different neighborhood name based on whether the event was good or bad), unquestioned, and damaging; and she has ideas about how we can un-hide them and change the dialogue about the city.

Becky telescopes us out to show that the defaults about Chicago among non-Chicagoans (Al Capone and the ghetto) and those about specific areas of Chicago are often built up and passed along by people who've never been. And she points to the power of a trusted source (people who have actually been there) to break the chain and show people that the city won't eat you alive.

Halle's unusually integrated high school experience set her up to spot the defaults – because she didn't understand them (wait, *why* am I supposed to hate Black people?). As an adult living in Chicago, she's heard all the exaggerated defaults from family (you went to the Sox game last night? Everything ok?) and friends reacting to her decision to teach at a community college on the South Side. Caroline, a White woman living in a Black neighborhood largely because she wasn't opposed to it (not because she actively sought it), casts into sharp relief the array of exaggerated warnings she and her friends have experienced; who can ever forget "jaws of death," "it's your funeral" and "do you have a death wish" doled out by police officers to the White person who ventures into a Black neighborhood?

Other defaults are not so blatant. Jamaine's story is full of the dog whistles (another form of shortcuts) blown by potential roommates, classmates, family members in New York, and online housing search tools to steer people (him) away from Black spaces.

His own housing search was made tiring by these whistles and his social life with his classmates in urban planning was strained by their reluctance to go to Black neighborhoods (even as they studied them in their classes).

Halle – and many other of our storytellers – share a common personality trait that came up time and time again in our interviews. Some version of being the kind of person who "goes against the status quo" or "likes to see things for themselves" or "is a contrarian." And we're glad they did, because we are witnessing the lessons learned and opportunities opened when people are willing to un-hide the shortcuts. In fact, in the next section, we will meet Kristine, who gave us some great language for this endeavor: she captures the task at hand when she says "I want to change my default on what I think about South and West Side neighborhoods."

Don't Go is about helping everyone – contrarians and non-contrarians alike – work to discover and counter these damaging shortcuts – to change their defaults about the city's neighborhoods. And to Go. And for those worried about being a "tourist" when they go? First of all, don't go snapping photos of people you don't know. But also, be committed to seeing things differently. If you're just going to a place without being aware of your confirmation bias – your tendency to see what you think you'll see – then no, it won't work to just volunteer or visit. But if you can see the Don't Go mentality you've been raised to believe, and you aim to "change your default" view of Black neighborhoods, then you'll make some progress.

Maria: Avoiding the shortcuts takes work. And it takes more work when the information is hard to come by – think of Jerry's story of having to find alternative information sources from the local paper, because they don't cover all of the city – and especially not Black neighborhoods. As a social scientist, this makes me think of what decision scientists and behavioral economists have to say about how humans make complex decisions. These are big scholarly fields, so I won't go into the details[9] but just pick out two points they make about decisions: (1) we try for the cognitively easiest way to do it – we use shortcuts (or, as decision scientists call them, heuristics); and (2) we are impacted by "choice architecture,"[10] which means that how our choices are presented to us can have a big impact on what decisions we make. Both of these ideas mean that when we are making decisions, we don't process all the possible information and then make "rational" decisions like a computer. Left to our own devices, we generally rely on the easiest way (using shortcuts) to make a decision. And because of segregation, the easiest decisions are often ones that segregate us. So that means we have to make special efforts to do something different. To not use a default. To break out of our bubbles. This makes me think of how Tonika, at the beginning of all of our interviews, would ask for our storytellers' Instagram handles, so she could follow them and "mess with her algorithms." The social media equivalent of "work hard" to find what they don't want you to find.

Tonika: For my part, as someone born and bred in Englewood, I appreciate the effort this takes. Our conversation with Jenny made me think about something that happened during the time we have been doing this project. There was a shooting a few blocks behind my house. Apparently, the people involved were running past our street at 3 in the morning. I found a bullet hole in my trunk the next day and I felt really conflicted. But I feel like it's important to say this because this situation is really complex. My street is quiet and normal and a great place to grow up and live, but there is gang activity and other stuff that causes certain blocks or addresses in my neighborhood to be less safe at certain times.

But there's a big difference between saying "don't go" to Englewood and "be mindful at this time in this certain area of Englewood because there was an incident here recently or something is happening here, and the situation is not fully resolved." The latter indicates empathy and concern while the former conveys disdain and sometimes maybe sympathy but not empathy. In other words, not the idea that this happened in a neighborhood where "good" people just like you live. So I appreciate the way Jenny offered a way to explain this to people. That she was willing to dive into the complexity instead of just saying everything is great or everything is awful.

Neither is true at any time about any neighborhood anywhere, including mine.

Section 4
From Hurt to Healing

ACCORDINGLY – LESLIE'S STORY

I WAS PART OF THE 2019 OBAMA FOUNDATION COMMUNITY Leadership Corps Program. Tonika was one of the first speakers to our group, and she asked us to indicate our home-towns by pushing a pin onto a map at the front of the room.

I remember feeling so conflicted. I grew up impoverished. Folks like us tend to move around a lot. I was like,

"Where do I belong?

Where do I put this pin?"

In the presentation, Tonika talked about leaving her home in Englewood at 5:45 a.m. to catch a bus so she could be at Lane Tech High School on the North Side by 8 a.m. Every school day for four years.

Tonika talked about seeing the differences in the landscape as she traveled up north. That's something I had to do too. I took a long drive every morning with my older sister from my home on the Southwest Side of Chicago to Mozart Elementary School on the Northwest Side of Chicago. That's when I saw the differences in race and class and how everything was structured.

We moved around a lot, so I got to see how different everyone was and how people talked about different spaces. That's partly why I studied sociology. I just found it so interesting that people always start by asking you,

"So, where are you from?"

Then, they treat you accordingly.

Sometimes I felt like I was paranoid or something, like I was reading too much into this. But college changed that.

When I got to Concordia University Chicago in 2012, I was like, oh my goodness. I'm here. I'm in college. This is unreal to me. My mom wasn't able to get a lot of education growing up, and my family had to work really hard to make ends meet. Little me was nerding out at college orientation – I even brought my mom and grandma to see it. It was really cool.

Eventually, we sat outside on the ground in small circles and the tour guides started asking questions to help us get to know one another better. Like,

"Who's traveled to more than one country before?"

Lots of people are raising their hands. I was like,

"Whoa."

I started to feel more and more out of place.

"What's your favorite brand?"

And students were saying really expensive brands. Right then and there, people were fighting to say they were pretty well-off. I didn't realize how much of a difference there was between me and them. It got to a point where I realized,

"I'm *really* poor."

The imposter syndrome was starting to form in my mind. I felt really out of place.

I didn't know this at the time, but my address told people how they should talk to me, about me, and at me

After I aced the math placement tests, I mingled with a group of other Latinx students from the North Side. We had never met. And as soon as I said that I grew up in Humboldt Park and that I lived now in Cicero, I was categorized as an outsider, as a danger-ous person from "the 'hood." The students from the North Side told me their parents said my neighborhoods were dangerous. And that's why their families don't live "out there." They said the news is always covering areas like mine.

I didn't know this at the time, but my address told people how they should talk to me, about me, and at me. Suddenly, I felt that this power was created for better-off Latinx and POC [person of color] families who came into the US the "right way" or who had a better social class. And for them this translated into how hard their parents worked not to live "where all the Mexicans lived," on the West or the South Side.

In other words, they were able to "afford" diversity. Another layer is added on if you talk about what schools you come from; I was looked at like a wild child for coming from Chicago Public Schools (CPS) instead of a private school or charter schools. They were so surprised to learn I had aced my math placement – because it complicated what they thought they knew about CPS and the West Side.

I did not complete the orientation that night with my new class-mates. I went home to regroup and come back the next morning for the first day of classes. Everyone else went downtown to do a scavenger hunt and they slept in the dorms. I felt grateful to get away. My classmates from the North Side would say,

"Oh, you're from down there."

I was like,

"What do you mean?"

And they would say,

"Well, I see every single night that there are shootings over there. You're from over there? And that's where you're living?"

It was this disbelief. This question – "How are you surviving every single day?" Like this assumption that my block was unliv-able. That I was surrounded by constant violence.

Another thing, too, is being brushed off. When they found out where I was from, the other students weren't as curious about me. They didn't ask me real questions, they just made assumptions about my life, and about how smart I was (or wasn't).

I just think that it's something people know, but it's not something people talk about. I'm not trying to call people out. But we shouldn't think this about each other. And so that's why I was really interested in this project. Chicago is very segregated, and we don't talk about it enough. Chicago's segregation is just seen as normal.

I remember my first Latinx professor in college. She said,

"Doesn't it ever bother y'all that the city is segregated?"

That always stuck with me, because it reminded me of the car rides to school where I saw it.

Some of the White people on campus would say things that made me uncomfortable. I remember walking up to a group of classmates and being like,

"Hey, what are y'all doing?"

And they were like,

"Oh, Leslie, are you feeling spicy?"

And they were all really friendly and close to one another. I was like,

"Hey, you don't want to get me mad."

Then they were like,

"You gonna shank me?"

So I was like,

"Ah, ok, I need to go back to my room, this is just too much."

That's just how White people thought of Latinx people in Chicago. They assumed things about me. I had a classmate tell me I was the first Latinx person they had talked to in real life. That the only things they knew were from seeing Latinx people on TV!

Then as I progressed into my sociology classes, I thought,

"Why are we like this?

Why don't we talk about these things?

Why don't we try and hang out with people from different neighborhoods?"

I would challenge my friends to come to the West Side. When I was a Resident Advisor, I remember trying to get the residents to explore Chicago – like once I tried to get them to go with me to Chinatown. But they were utterly afraid to leave the campus in the suburbs.

It was always a struggle. I was like,

"Why don't we interact with each other?"

I know it's hard to interact because of the way Chicago is set up but I just think it's really important to name the elephant.

Sometimes, I can be more direct.

If people make comments about where I grew up, I'll say,

"I don't know where you heard that,"

or I'll just try and toss it back onto them like,

"I don't know what you mean. It's not at all like what you think. You should come and visit."

I just feel like it's really important to touch on these painful issues because I always feel like we're dancing around it. Sometimes I just want to cut through it and just ask,

"What are you really trying to say?"

Other times I just ask directly,

"What do you really mean by that?"

How do we get folks to understand how it feels when they react differently to people from different places?

I know that can be a very pointed question. But at the same time, I don't know why we let this slide anymore. How do we get more folks to feel like a fish out of water, so that they can understand how our interactions are class-based and race-based? How do we get folks to understand how it feels when they react differently to people from different places?

I just want to ask people,

"Do you really want to know about me, or do you want to just confirm what you've been told about people like me?"

ENGINEERING CHANGE – TIANA'S STORY

YOU KNOW, I REALLY DIDN'T HAVE TIME TO DO THIS INTER- view, but I was like, this is the time to do it. This is the time for people to get out of their own box and figure out what the rest of the world is about.

We used to call my uncle the lecturer. He would sit us down and say,

"Look, this is how the world is. When you get older, you know people are gonna discriminate against you. You always got to be good. Make sure you get your education. You always got to be better."

We would try to run away whenever my uncle arrived, but he always made my cousins and all of us sit down and listen, again. We would tell him,

"We got it, we got it. We got it already!" But recently I told my uncle,

"Man, *everything* you said was true. Everything."

I was born and raised in Englewood. I lived in my grandma's house with my mom, my twin brother, and my little sister. My grandparents (and many of the people on our block) were some of the first Black families to buy homes in Englewood, so there were lots of older people and families who had lived there for a long time, which made my childhood pretty great.

I attended what used to be called Altgeld Elementary School, located at 71st and Loomis and graduated valedictorian of my class. When I attended Dunbar Vocational High School, I got more and more interested in computers, science, and math. I had my choice of colleges that accepted me, but my Uncle Elliot always told me IIT was the place to go for engineering. Besides, Dunbar was close and I never saw anyone that looked like me at IIT when I walked around it. So I vowed to maybe be the one person that somebody might see and say,

"Hey, I can go there. I see someone there who is just like me. I can go to IIT too." Maybe I can be what I was looking for.

I remember seeing Tonika's post where she asked a group of first-year students at Northwestern if they had ever been told, "Don't go." Seeing that almost all of the students raised their hands brought back memories of my freshman year at IIT.

On my first day as a student there in 2000, I remember thinking,

"Any ethnicities that you can think of are here!" I was excited to learn about new cultures.

The first Black person I met that day was from Zimbabwe and she had an English accent because she grew up in London. I was beyond intrigued. I was the first Black person she met on orientation day too. She ended up hanging out with me and my mom for the whole day and we are still friends now.

The three of us attended a parent orientation event together, where my mom and I were shocked (to say the very least) when the presenters told the whole auditorium of mostly White and International students that

it is NOT safe to ride the Red Line

and

Don't go east of Michigan Avenue, north of 31st Street, south of 35th Street, or west of the Dan Ryan Expressway.

I remember seeing my mom's face change as she said, "So, they basically just told people not to leave campus? Not even to travel around the city?"

The people on stage at the orientation basically told a room full of newcomers to Chicago not to go to our neighborhoods because it was unsafe

This was the first time I ever heard anything like this. I've always lived on the South Side, and I did go to places outside of my neighborhood. We didn't have any real money to spend, but my mom took us downtown so that we could walk around the Water Tower and do other stuff like that. But I never heard anyone say anything like,

"Don't go to the South Side."

My mom was just disgusted. The people on stage at the orientation basically told a room full of newcomers to Chicago not to go to our neighborhoods because it was unsafe.

IIT is a heavily international school, so they were saying this to people from Australia, India, and Africa. They were saying this to people from all over the world. And only about 2 or 3% of the student population at that time was Black American, so you can imagine how my mom and I felt. Why would they tell people that?

I remember walking through the streets outside of the campus, looking at the brownstones, just amazed at how huge and beautiful the houses were. I felt so disheartened when I would hear people talk about Bronzeville and other South Side neighborhoods like they were trash or some terrible, unsafe place to be.

I did my best to defend the South Side while I was at IIT. By the time I went to college, my mom and my siblings had moved to a two-bedroom apartment in Englewood, a few blocks from my childhood home. I started bringing friends home with me for Thanksgiving who couldn't go home for break. One of my friends from India was vegetarian and I remember my mom saying that's ok. We got you. We had collard greens, dressing and vegetables for her.

None of us had cars, so we rode the bus there together. Then instead of spending the night at my mom's house, I took the bus back to campus with my friends, so they felt safe while traveling in an unfamiliar city. It was important to me that they saw parts of the South Side experience that is rarely shown.

After I graduated from IIT in 2004 with a B.S. in Electrical Engineering, I had to defend the South Side at work too. In my field, I am often the only Black person, and I am almost always the only Black woman in a workspace or at an event.

Some years ago, I received an award at a work banquet. I was seated with a couple who were new to the Chicagoland area, and I asked them where they were planning to live. They told me they were thinking about some neighborhoods on the North Side. The company I worked for was in Indiana, south of Chicago, so the North Side would be a long commute.

I said that maybe they should check out Beverly and the Morgan Park area on the South Side. That's when they told me they had been advised to stay away from the South Side. This couple was from another country, but someone had already told them not to go to the South Side. I'm betting that the person who offered that bit of "wisdom" never stepped foot on the South Side of Chicago.

I feel like the people who have the most to say about the South Side have never been there. But they probably got the idea from the news. So, it's like a self-perpetuating stereotype about a whole area of Chicago. You read or hear about some bad thing happening on the South or the West Side, and then you tell people they shouldn't live there. Then those people stay away, and they advise other people to stay away. Until I saw the Folded Map exhibit, I never thought about how spreading these lies actually perpetuates segregation in the city.

I still try to speak up for the South Side and I help people go there. I'll say,

"Well, if you're nervous about going to a particular neighborhood, I'll go with you. Let's take a walk/ride."

You know, a number of people that we met at that IIT orientation had never been around a Black person before.

Just imagine that.

You've never been around a certain group.

You watch or listen to or read the news or scroll through your social media bubble, which tells you to stay away from that group.

Then, the leaders at your school tell you not to leave the campus because the surrounding area is dangerous.

You notice that it's mostly Black and Brown people who reside in that area.

So what makes that area dangerous? It must be the people, of course.

Therefore, Black and Brown people must be dangerous, right??

Then you tell your friends and family to stay away from neighborhoods like mine. They tell their friends and family to stay away too.

This cycle exacerbates racist views and instills prejudice in generation after generation of people.

Because people and companies stay away, neighborhoods don't get the funding they need and so the disinvestment grows worse, which feeds into the idea that the neighborhood is dangerous and/or desolate.

I will always try to speak up. Even now, I am wearing my South Side-proud T-shirt. I can't help myself.

So, when people say anything bad about the South Side, I'm usually like,

"Who told you that? Have you ever been there? Or are you just going off somebody's word-of-mouth? Come with me. I'll take you around."

I will always try to speak up. Even now, I am wearing my South Side-proud T-shirt. I can't help myself

I definitely talk about how proud I am to have grown up on the South Side. And I say,

"The South Side made me who I am."

I don't divulge it easily all the time though. Usually, if somebody asked me where I grew up, I say,

"I grew up on the South Side." And they say,

"Oh, the South Side, where?"

Then I'll say,

"Oh, I grew up in Englewood."

And they're like, REALLY?

And I say,

"Guess what, there are a lot of us that are successful from Englewood and neighborhoods like it."

Then they say,

"No, you're one of the different ones."

And I'm like,

"No, *those people* are just like me. *Those people* are me. And I am like them. Do you get it? I AM them."

At some point, it gets tiring. I guess you could say that I have to defend myself all the time. And sometimes it's not worth it. Many people automatically assume that people from the neighborhoods that are labeled "BAD" are "BAD" people.

Now, you have some people, they're going to think what they think, and they have no interest in changing. They choose not to pay attention to how Black people are treated and have no desire to dig into why these inequities exist. Because there is NO WAY that you don't know that Black people are treated differently. That's a kind of blissful ignorance – If I don't completely see it with my own eyes, I don't have to believe it's true.

But since 2020, people are open to having the conversation about these differences. My energy is renewed by all the protests and conversations. I think this is perfect timing for Folded Map and for this project. People are more open to explore. And even if they don't physically go to the communities, they're more open to learning about why these neighborhoods are the way they are. I feel like people are finally open to learning about our experiences and about our neighborhoods.

I hope real change will come.

Then I can share my pride in my heritage, without constantly defending myself and the South Side, and without constantly telling people I am NOT an exception to some stupid made-up "rule."

FROM MAD MAX TO LADY
DATES – KRISTINE'S STORY

A T ONE POINT I THOUGHT,
"I am like a super woke liberal person.
I went on the anti-gentrification bus tours."

Then in 2006, I volunteered to help with an international design competition for a playlot in West Garfield Park, and I met a Black woman from the neighborhood. She was like,

"Oh, please, come gentrify my neighborhood. I've lived here for so long. I own this property and I would love for my property rates to go up." And I was like,

"Well, huh."

This is more complicated than I thought. Garfield Park wasn't a monolith after all. Here was a woman who lived in a not-great neighborhood. But she was a professional. She was very active in her community. She probably could have afforded to move out, but she chose to live here anyway. And so it was interesting to me.

I've been taught my whole life that people are trying to get out of these "bad" neighborhoods. But once you spend time there, you actually see the place, and it's like,

"Oh, no, there's real value here." That was really eye-opening.

So I started asking myself,

217

"Did I feel uncomfortable in these places?"

No, I actually didn't.

I don't really consider myself that great of an ally. I am sort of a typical middle-aged White lady who lives on the North Side. I have some friendly acquaintances that are Black or POC. But I don't live a very integrated life.

My whole life, I've been told:

"It's NOT safe for White people to be in Garfield Park."

But honestly, if a White person got shot every time they walked into Garfield Park or Bronzeville or Englewood, that would be all over the news, right?

It doesn't happen that way. In fact, the people from these neighborhoods were overwhelmingly kind to me, maybe even more welcoming than the people from my neighborhood in Ukrainian Village.

Meeting that woman from Garfield Park was sort of like the spark for me.

I got the opportunity to work on an architecture project in Altgeld Gardens, a public housing project on the South Side managed by the Chicago Housing Authority.

I expected the reaction I got from my parents, with my dad saying,

"Hey, is that place really safe?" and my mom saying,

"Be careful."

But I was surprised by one of my friends who said,

"Oh, Altgeld Gardens, that's like an open-air drug market."

Then another one of my friends said,

"You think YOU'RE going to fix THAT? Obama couldn't fix THAT."

I think, as White people, we look at some of these neighborhoods as if we're supposed to fix them. As if our presence in them is supposed to be uplifting, this wonderful benefit to the people who live there. Like,

Now White people want to come in your neighborhood, so Bronzeville has finally made it!

And that's not the solution either. So, I don't know, that's one of the things that I wrestle with, and why I feel like I'm almost a tourist in these neighborhoods. I'm trying to figure out if that's beneficial or not.

Trayvon Martin's murder in 2012 definitely made me think:

"Am I this person who thinks of Black people that way?

How am I looking at people?

Would I be calling the police?

How would I approach somebody that was different in my neighborhood?"

I distinctly remember thinking,

"We have to do better." And I was a little more conscious about how I was interacting, how I was noticing Black people in my space.

If I saw a Black person on the street in my predominantly White neighborhood, what was I thinking about what this person was doing?

Am I giving that person the benefit of the doubt?

I have friends who are reposting every Black Lives Matter meme and resources and every GoFundMe and that's good. But I'm also like,

"Okay, so you're doing this. Great. But have you ever been on Madison Street? Have you ever gone for ribs on 43rd Street?"

I don't think so.

So I thought my story might be interesting, because the way that I interact with the city is a little different. But still, I'm almost like a tourist when I go on the South and West Sides. I'm going there for a specific destination. I'm going there to explore something that isn't in my neighborhood.

That's why I went to Tonika's Folded Map exhibit in Englewood in 2018. I wanted to explore the depth of my interactions with neighborhoods that aren't mine. I realized that it's not out of fear that I don't go now. It's more of a feeling that I'm just visiting. That I'm not really a part of this.

I do love the Garfield Park Conservatory and one of my favorite things to do is take a friend. It's such a good lady date place. We hit the Conservatory, and then find some great food on Madison or, you know, go over to Life Kitchen or one of those places.

What worries me is that as a visitor, I don't feel like I'm actually engaging in these neighborhoods

So I'm exposing a friend to a new community and supporting a neighborhood economically. That is always a good thing. And every time I've been to a soul food restaurant on Madison, or what have you, people have just been so welcoming. Those are good things, just seeing that there's places and there's value in these neighborhoods that other people maybe aren't seeing. So you can't just system-wide say,

"Just scratch everything west of Kimball and south of Roosevelt and have it be done." Because there's wonderful people to meet and things to see and do all over the city.

What worries me is that as a visitor, I don't feel like I'm actually engaging in these neighborhoods. Whereas if I went to, say, the cathedral and then to dinner in Edison Park on the North Side, I don't feel like a visitor. I'm part of it in a way that maybe I'm not in these other neighborhoods. Everyone is welcoming and very polite and all that, but I feel disconnected. If I were a regular somewhere, you know, if I got to know an ice cream shop or coffee shop or whatever and frequented it, I wouldn't have that same feeling. I don't want it to be like,

I am going to the South Side to see this Black neighborhood.

That's not helpful, either. I want to interact. I want to get local perspectives. I want to try new experiences. And I don't know another way to do that other than physically be in that space. I struggle with it. Because I'm just like,

Am I helping? Or is it . . .? I don't know. I wouldn't like to say that eating ribs on the South Side is performative, but I don't usually post my visits on social media, because that just feels like I'm saying, "Look At Me, A White Lady Eating Ribs On The South Side."

I drove Lyft for a while. In Andersonville and Logan Square, I found myself competing with lots of other drivers. I would sit in an empty car for hours. But on the South Side?

My car was never empty. Other drivers complained about the shorter rides if you stayed on the South Side. They said,

"We don't want to make 2 dollars here and there."

But there's a big bucket that a driver gets paid the minute somebody hails. So even though my rides were short, I made more money per hour.

If I could tell the other drivers anything, I would say,

"You're gonna let your fear of the South Side keep you from making more money? You're just gonna drive around Lincoln Park and have your car be empty half the time when you can make good money?"

People ask me,

"Don't you feel unsafe?" And I'm like,

"No."

Look, if every third person were getting raped and murdered in a Lyft or Uber, this system wouldn't work. You can't have a neighborhood of you know, tens of thousands of people, and assume everybody's bad. That would just be post-apocalyptic.

It's not like you drive down to Englewood and suddenly,

"It's Mad Max and the Thunderdome!"

It's quite the opposite. That's what I think is just so crazy about some of these perceptions. I'm like,

"Man, if you just physically drove down there."

Rideshare on the South Side was a whole fascinating world. People apologized to me for making me drive to their neighborhood at three o'clock on a Saturday afternoon. It's almost like the people from these neighborhoods have had so many experiences where drivers were ticked off about being taken outside of downtown or Logan Square or whatever. And that just made me sad. I mean, like three-quarters of the city shouldn't be apologizing to middle-aged White ladies or anyone else for where they live or where they work.

I wasn't worried about somebody breaking into my Honda Fit. I wasn't afraid of being mugged during my 40-foot walk across the street. Because if it happened that way, the South Side and the West Side would be a wasteland. And they're not. You just have to drive by. You'll see block clubs and people out and about, and you would maybe think differently. That's what's so interesting to me.

Some of the danger is actually what you're bringing with you

As soon as I was comfortable driving on the South and West Sides, my passengers stopped apologizing. And then I got even more comfortable, so I started to ask for tips on the best places to go and other stuff. One guy I drove out to West Garfield Park was wearing chef gear, so we started talking about food. And he told me about a great place to eat. So you just break down those walls and show that you're not afraid. Then it's like,

"Hey, we are just two people in a car."

Then you get to see what makes these neighborhoods great.

Some of the danger is actually what you're bringing with you.

Those perceptions that you bring with you are causing things. So if you go down to the South Side and

you're clutching your purse, and

222

you're only going to go to this one place in Pilsen, or

you're afraid to wander the beach,

I think it's not that people pick up on the fear, they pick up on the fact that you're unfriendly and you don't want to engage with people. And I think that's important. One way to break down that sort of tourist feeling is to have actual conversations with people when you're in those neighborhoods.

I volunteered with My Block, My Hood, My City a couple times to help decorate the neighborhood with lights for the winter holiday season. That was really fun. I especially loved the block club sign project they were also doing at the time. My Block, My Hood, My City partnered with another organization to redesign the signs. I loved that so much because I was like,

Oh man, I, as a White person, am surrounded by positivity. My community garden is a place of love and whatever. I exist in this land of positivity.

On the South Side though, the signs were all like warnings. No littering, no this and no that. So l liked the positive ways they changed the messages on the block club signs. The old signs supported the typical misperceptions of these communities. Over the years, what I've been trying to do is *change my default on what I think about South and West Side neighborhoods.*

I lived in Hazel Crest on the South Side until I was in fourth grade. My family and I moved from the south suburbs to a northwestern suburb "for the schools."

Since my grandparents and extended family lived in the city, we frequently visited Chicago after we moved, but we held onto our fear.

I remember when I met my parents for lunch to celebrate my first job at an architecture firm in River North. I noticed that my mom was clutching her purse while she was talking to a Black man. She was very nice to his face, but you could see by her body language that she was afraid. And I was like,

"You know, this is just a poor person who probably doesn't have a home. He's not stealing anything. He's just asking for money."

And my mom responded by reminding me that she was raised in the city, and I was raised in the suburbs, so I was naïve.

My mother is a sweet, sweet lady. One-on-one, she is just such a wonderful, engaging person. But she has these thoughts that are just really systemically damaging. And so, I think I need to be putting myself in more places where I feel uncomfortable.

I think we're all unpacking things in the wake of, frankly, this confluence of . . . I mean, let's be honest: The difference between this time and Freddie Gray or any number of other police brutality situations, is that we all have time on our hands, because we're home alone and thinking about these things. And I'm hoping that this is just a big evolution point in America, and in our culture, and in the city of Chicago. Because we need to do something. We need to make things better. And that means we've got to change our behaviors. And that means we've got to change our thoughts.

I've had some really fascinating conversations with my mom, in part because we've run out of things to talk about, since we're talking every day, and none of us are doing anything. So we've had some really gut-wrenching conversations about like,

"Okay, why do you think this? What does this mean to you?" And my mom still keeps saying to me that I'm a liberal and an idealist. And that's why I think these things.

I told her, "the only way we break out of that is by physically experiencing places that aren't our own, that are challenging to our concept of life. And being open to a new experience."

My mom has come a lot further than I expected, but she's still a little like, well, you're naïve, you don't have the experiences I do. And then I'm like,

"Well you don't have the experiences I do, either."

I've had a lot more success recently because my previous tack was like,

"You're wrong. You need to get over yourself."

I've done a lot more listening now. And asking questions. And the discussions have come a lot further because I think she feels less dismissed.

In fact, I've convinced her that when things are open again, we're going to go to the Garfield Park Conservatory for a great lady date.

CURIOSITY PASSPORTS –
ROBERTO'S STORY

THE QUESTION THAT WE SHOULD ASK PEOPLE IS "WHAT MAKES you not be curious? Whenever did you stop asking questions, and whenever did the fear and being scared become stronger than love, and stronger than curiosity, and stronger than fun, just to get to know somebody that was different. Just to see what's up."

What makes people so afraid of people who look different, speak different, wear different things from them? I feel children are the most curious things. I mean, kids are constantly asking questions and going places and asking dumb questions and all that. And I think at some point, people start telling them,

"DON'T talk about that!

Don't ask her that question.

Don't touch that.

Don't do that.

Don't do that!"

The question is, when do we start not being who we are? Because the essence of a human being is to be curious. "Oh, who is she? What's going on? Why do you look different? What's up with that dress? And what's up with that?" I feel that's a natural state.

I think the unnatural state is to see somebody who is completely different and be like, Okay, and just not acknowledge the difference. I think healing is about going back to your inner child or whatever that little part of you is, that child asking questions.

And that child is not afraid of asking someone who doesn't look like them:

"Where are you from?"

The question is, when do we start not being who we are? Because the essence of a human being is to be curious

I'm sure there's studies about the moment when kids start to pick up on their parent's crap and I think while some parts of my childhood were quashed, for sure, that part was never crushed. The part that asks people questions and feels more interested in the different person. Because the rest of you? I already know you. There's nothing else you need to tell me. I get you.

But this guy is new, I want to know what's up with him.

I went to my new roommate's birthday party the day I arrived from my home country of Spain in 2001. After her birthday party downtown, she took me to see Lake Michigan.

I thought the lake looked like the ocean. I thought Chicago was amazing.

Then I was told NOT to take the CTA to Chicago State University.

I'd moved four or five thousand miles from my home. I was here to learn from people who are different from me. For 25 years I'd been surrounded by people like me that look like me, speak like me. But here I could learn about the history of the Native American, African American, Asian, and Latino communities. I could learn about all the different nationalities within Latin America, and all the different groups within the Black community.

But that wasn't how Chicago was set up to work at all. To the contrary, I was told to curb my enthusiasm and keep my questions at a minimum, because this is not what we're about here. We're not about sharing who we are, exchanging cultures, and all that. We are about finding our place in the box and staying there within that box.

I was still in Spain when I was matched up with my roommate, who posted an ad seeking a native Spanish speaker who could teach her Spanish. So I basically moved in with a stranger to Logan Square, where I was immediately told:

"Don't go to the West Side of Logan Square – that's where the Puerto Ricans are!"

But I'm here to learn. I'm a student. I moved very far because I wanted to learn. Why are you all making this so complicated?

When I needed a textbook that was only available at Chicago State University, my classmates told me "DON'T GO." And going to 95th and State created commotion in my little group of friends.

"What in the hell are you going to Chicago State University for? Are you sure you're not going to University of Chicago?"

No, I'm going there because I need a book that is in their library.

"Why would you go all the way there for a book? Can't you just buy it?"

Yeah, I can buy it, but I have no money. I'm a student, they have it there, and I like seeing neighborhoods.

Behind all those questions was the concern that the 95th St. station area was problematic in terms of crime.

I did ask my professor about this. I said,

"You know, I hate to ask you this question. I feel ashamed to ask this question. But I feel like my life is in danger right now over a trip that I'm taking to a neighborhood that I'm pretty sure thousands of people live in every day. People are telling me to not go there."

And she told me, "I'm pretty sure that if you don't mess with people, people won't mess with you."

That's what I thought too.

So I went. I didn't feel danger. I did get questioned a few times. People were trying to be helpful though, not accusatory. As soon as I start speaking with my Spanish accent, people genuinely felt concerned that I was supposed to be on the side of the tracks going to the North Side.

"What are you doing here? Are you sure you're in the right place? Are you okay?"

I remember walking to the library at Chicago State University and feeling sadness about the vacant space. Some people were selling really cheap stuff in the streets. The neighborhood was obviously disinvested, but I didn't feel any danger. I got my book, went back home, and then I went back again to return the book.

After living in Chicago for 20 years, Tonika's artistic work prompted me to reflect on the seemingly simple question she posed: Have you been told "Don't Go"?

When I started to think about it, all my life, every day almost, people have been telling me directly or indirectly: Don't go there.

I had to walk west one night after class. The custodian at the school warned me about walking through the ABLA Homes public housing project.

"No vayas. Ten cuidado con los morenos en los proyectos.

Don't go. Be careful with the Black people in the projects."

Of course there is racism in what the janitor said, but at least he had the honesty of telling me exactly what he thought about it. There was this directness of saying, you need to know that I feel strongly that you need to be very careful around Black people in public housing. I will never forget that.

My first job was monitoring the CHA Plan for Transformation. So I have met many people who live and work in Chicago public housing. Never in my entire career did I feel like I had to be "careful" around Black people from a Chicago public housing project. Not once.

And of course there is a lot of privilege because obviously the people who are worried about going to a Black neighborhood are the people who have the least reason to be worried about going to a Black neighborhood.

The point of my job is to know what's going on in Chicago communities. If you isolate me in a car, I miss half of what's going on. I miss the real world.

But people STILL say:

"You shouldn't have gone alone. You shouldn't have taken the train!"

People are well-intentioned. They are trying to protect me. I know this, and I am not sure how to explain the harm caused by their concerns.

At the time I moved here, there was no orientation about race at all. So I had to kind of piece things together and ask a lot of dumb questions and weird questions in class and outside of class. My friends would tell me,

"Sometimes you ask questions that are too direct, maybe tone it down a bit."

But I was asking about pretty obvious things, like:

"Why were almost all the people who drove and took care of the CTA buses Black?

Why were almost all the administrative assistants at the university Black?

Why were almost all the professors and high-level administrators at the university White?"

A lot of people didn't feel comfortable answering those questions in public, even in my school. So I learned that curiosity is great. You got to start from a place of curiosity. But when it comes to race in the United States, you have to be very respectful and careful because you may be hurting people when you ask questions. And if you ask a question too harshly, you kind of rehash issues for a Black person or a Latino student or hurt them by this directness that you have.

I also realized my privilege, being an international student. I have this passport because I was a foreigner and I got away with stuff. I could ask questions. And even if they were sometimes dumb and asinine, and even hurtful, they would give me the pass of you know, he doesn't know any better. Let's have a conversation with him. But no one else felt compelled to ask those questions. Or very few people were asking the questions.

So, on the one hand, I had this message that was,

"Be careful what you ask and how you ask it and when you ask it."

But at the same time, the message that came very often was,

"Thank you for asking that. Thank you for the question. Because no one is asking the question."

> ## And then I realized that nobody knew how to do this well. And nobody knows now. So all you can do is try your best not to harm people in finding the truth

So it was very difficult for somebody with very little clue at the beginning to navigate this. Okay, so you want me to ask the questions, but ask the questions differently. You don't want to tell me more about that because you feel uncomfortable talking about this. So help me out.

And then I realized that nobody knew how to do this well. And nobody knows now. So all you can do is try your best not to harm people in finding the truth. All you can do is try your best to dismantle all the stuff that is preventing people from being free, being themselves, having access and being able to ask the questions of themselves.

One thing that was shocking to me is how many people in Chicago had been to my country, to Spain. They went to Madrid, Barcelona, to a university in Spain, but they have never been to Woodlawn, Englewood, or Garfield Park.

When they discover I'm from Spain, Chicagoans often ask me what I like about Chicago. I tell them I love the neighborhoods – but people often confess to me that they have never been to the neighborhoods I have visited. Then I say,

"Well, that could change tomorrow. You don't need a passport or a plane."

It's $2.50 for the CTA. So one thing that needs to happen, I think, is for people to spend more quality time in communities that are not their community.

You'll discover by day three that it's like your neighborhood, but just in another part of town. Same people. Same issues (but less economic opportunity).

Walk a mile in the shoes of a person from a disinvested neighborhood. Treat yourself to a "gym membership" for anti-racism. See what it actually feels like.

"How would YOU feel?

You, from Lincoln Park?

Or you, from Arlington Heights?

Or you, from some other White suburb?

If every day you open the newspaper, turn on the TV, watch a show, and your community and the people who look like you and your family members are constantly shown depicted with words like

Downtrodden, criminals, SHOOTING, less-than, THUG!!!

Imagine they did that to you every single day.

Put yourself in those shoes.

How would YOU feel?"

I think especially White people go to this place where they feel like they are not responsible for this. They acknowledge that it's just a minority of Black people who are committing crimes, but then White people don't notice the minority of White people doing criminal things in their neighborhood (and trust me, there is a minority in your community committing crimes).

So imagine the reality. Imagine that there are criminal people in the White community, which is true. And now imagine that because of that little layer of people doing stuff up North, you and your family and your children and your wife and your friends are constantly seeing every time Arlington Heights shows up on TV, it's about crime, it's about what's wrong, it's about poverty.

Go inside the process: Let me feel what this human being may be feeling like. Let me walk for a moment in the shoes of somebody that is an artist or a professor or mailman or whatever.

And every day as he or she walks to and from work they get looked at in a certain way.

And imagine that happens for generation after generation.

On every channel, on every movie, on every newspaper, imagine that. People should do this exercise. Put themselves through a camp, where every day they wake up and people treat them like that.

Some people are too detached. They don't live there. They don't move there. They don't visit there. They just don't go.

Amy_Rey
@Amy_Rey

Writer, editor, feminist, anti-racist, crossword whiz. She/her pronouns.
bsky.app/profile/amyrey...

🔗 crosswordfiend.com   📅 Joined September 2008

QUESTIONS AND ANSWERS
– AMY'S STORY

WHITE PEOPLE GROW UP BEING TOLD, IF THERE'S A PROB-lem, you can turn to the police, and they will help you. White people are told that cops are there to serve and protect you.

So you've got a White woman who is growing up always thinking the cops are the good guys. And rules are there for a reason. Rules keep our society going. And then you see a little Black girl on the sidewalk selling her lemonade. If it were the White girl selling lemonade, you probably wouldn't have stopped to say, "Do you have a permit? I'm calling the cops." But you combine, "I like the cops and I like laws" with "I may have some concerns about people of color," and then you see a person of color who might be violating something, and you think, "well, this can't stand, this is a violation." Instead of just saying,

"Let me mind my own business."

People on Black Twitter explain that when a White person calls the cops on a Black person, the Black person faces a very real risk of ending up arrested or shot by the cops. It's not a neutral thing. Calling the cops is a very potent tool that White people have been using to control Black people for over 100 years. I'm sure you've both seen Ava DuVernay's documentary "13th." That was hugely educational and shocking to me. Like there was an awful lot that

I had no idea [about]. You know, Lincoln freed the slaves and then White people did everything they could to figure out how to throw a bunch of Black men into prison so that they can still be used for free labor. It's like, "all right, there's no slavery but we can still make it happen. We can do this."

> I would read advice from somebody saying, "Okay, if you are a White person and you're not understanding Black Lives Matter, or things like that, you need to actually get out there. Just follow some Black people on Twitter."

I don't know how I knew to follow Black Twitter, but every now and then I would read advice from somebody saying, "Okay, if you are a White person and you're not understanding Black Lives Matter, or things like that, you need to actually get out there. Just follow some Black people on Twitter."

I read books about race as well. I bought Ijeoma Oluo's book, *So You Want to Talk about Race*. But before her book came out, I read some of her long posts on social media. She wrote about going on a road trip out west with her kids. And they stopped at a Cracker Barrel in Colorado or Wyoming. She describes how she walked into the restaurant and was feeling apprehensive, like, "Are we going to get in trouble here?" Because it was an all-White area. And she ended up getting bombarded by White racists on Twitter saying *she* was racist for thinking that these White people might do them any harm. And it was like, thousands of people coming after her. And then maybe around six months ago when her teenage son was home alone sleeping, her house was hit with one of those SWAT attacks. Where somebody deliberately claims that some bad shit is going down at your address and calls the police there to terrorize you. So she had previously reported all these death threats and stuff that she had been getting to her local police in Seattle to let them know she might be at risk for these swatting attacks.

So she told them, "If you get a 911 call that claims somebody is being held hostage by a gunman in my house, know that it might be fake." Thank God they took that into account because her son gets woken up by the cops pounding on the door at two in the morning and it all went okay. He was terrified, but he wasn't physically harmed because these cops had been prepared that this might be a swatting thing as opposed to going in thinking, "Oh, God, this is a crisis, we need to be ready to shoot whoever comes to the door."

I can't believe the gall of these people calling her racist for posting about being afraid at Cracker Barrel. When my husband and I went on a road trip out west with his relatives, we were two Asians and two Whites. We felt nervous going into these small towns too.

So there's no real difference between Permit Patty making her call and somebody in the 1950s claiming that Emmett Till whistled at her and the people responding so viciously to Ijeoma Oluo. It's all just this long continuum.

After I learned about the danger posed by my white skin, I realized "Oh, when I'm walking down the street, and I pass a Black guy, maybe I should nod at him to let him know, Yes, I see you and I'm not going to call the cops on you." Like,

"I see that you're a person and I'm not afraid of you. And I'm not posing a threat to you because I'm not going to call the cops on you." And most of these men aren't even looking in my direction because, what have they been taught their whole lives?

Do you make eye contact with a White woman walking down the sidewalk if you're a Black man?

No, because then she's going to get scared and she's going to call the cops on you. Right?

So I'm like,

"All right, let me just make sure I don't look like I'm posing a danger to these guys. Because there are definitely people who do pose a danger to them, who they do need to be wary of."

When I'm walking down the street, and I pass a Black guy, maybe I should nod at him to let him know, Yes, I see you and I'm not going to call the cops on you

I grew up in south suburban Park Forest. My parents liked our Black neighbors (Park Forest was about 16% Black at the time), but everything in the culture told me that the South Side and the West Side of Chicago were dangerous, crime-ridden places. We were to try not to end up driving there. We knew not to get off the train before downtown (except maybe for Hyde Park, but you'd need to be careful even there). If you were going to be driving into the city, you had to be extra careful. Make sure you fill up the gas tank, check the oil, be sure about the directions, and LOCK the doors on the South Side. And if you encounter a Black man, or if you *might* encounter a Black man, you need to be on your guard. You need to double-check the locks. And don't EVER leave your car unlocked while you're driving or parking in a "bad" neighborhood. I think this was partly influenced by the news. The media wasn't about highlighting the good stuff, like "hey, there's a nice school program" or "hey, here's a really pretty garden." The news was always about crime, drugs, and poverty.

Even now, if you're taking a train up north, people "know" you shouldn't get off anywhere on the South Side of Chicago. Even though lots of people live there and they get on and off there all the time.

I unlearned a lot of what I was taught by following people on Black Twitter, especially men. Because I was hearing very human stories from Black men about the completely typical experiences they have. I follow comedian W. Kamau Bell. He is a Black man from Oakland, and he wears big hair. And he's very dark-skinned. He once went to a sidewalk cafe in Oakland, where he lives, and his wife and a friend of hers were there with his kid. He was bringing over a kid's book that he had just picked up at the bookstore and the restaurant staff thought he was some homeless dude coming to bother them. He was coming to talk to his wife through the window and the waitress was trying to shoo him away.

I also follow Elon James White. He is a Black man who lives in Oakland. He has a White wife and two little kids. He writes and talks about being hurt by people assuming things about him because he's a large Black guy. He started up this thing after his first kid was born – Daddy Game Proper – and he would get a bunch of other Black dads tweeting out pictures of themselves with their babies and their little kids. And you might see 50 pictures, a whole thread of young Black dads with their kids, and everybody's happy and healthy and normal and just doing family things. And it's like

"Okay, I see this. I see this and these are not scary men and there is no reason to think that they are scary men."

Now that I'm a middle-aged North Sider, I know that my family can drive through the South Side. I know that the risk is low for random outsiders, even when they're passing through neighborhoods with a lot of gang activity. I know the folks who live there (in the specific areas of those communities where gang activity is high) are the ones most at risk.

That my family can travel from South Lake Shore Drive all the way to the Dan Ryan, and nothing bad will happen. We can drive to the Garfield Park Conservatory on the West Side, and nothing bad will happen. We can drive out west to Westinghouse High School, and nothing bad will happen. My son can visit a friend in South Shore, and nothing bad will happen.

SAYING NO TO HATE –
JENNY S'S STORY

I DON'T THINK MY FEAR WENT AWAY OVERNIGHT. I'M SURE I WAS still thinking about it the next few times I went to Englewood. But having such a positive first-time experience under my belt helped. I feel like as a person, I don't always have the right words to express myself. I'm more intuitive. So I feel things deeply.

And I always feel a sense of rightness, and goodness, and love when we go to Englewood, so we spend a lot of time there.

I think relationships heal us. White supremacy teaches us that difference is a shame. White supremacy tells us we should fear people who are "different." This is especially harmful, because we are all different in some way from what society deems as perfectly normal. When we learn to love, celebrate, and honor the differences in others, we learn to love, celebrate, and honor the differences in ourselves.

I just think that when we truly love ourselves, there is no need to hate others

It's like the James Baldwin quote: "White people . . . have quite enough to do in learning how to accept and love themselves and each other, and when they have achieved this . . . the Negro problem will no longer exist, for it will no longer be needed."[11]

It seems like so many of our problems are rooted in this disconnection with our true selves; if we could connect to the energy of true and deep love for ourselves, that would manifest as love towards others.

I just think that when we truly love ourselves, there is no need to hate others.

When I tell people about my day, if it involved doing something in Englewood, Roseland, etc., I frequently get,

"Oh, that's so great that you are doing that, going there." As if I am being some kind of a hero for traveling to the South Side, a place many people I know and care about call home. People will also say,

"You took your kids?! Weren't you scared?"

It is an awful feeling to hear that. People never say that about Lakeview. And I am always self-conscious about being perceived as or acting like a White savior. I have asked a Black friend of mine,

"Do you think that about me? That I am a White savior person?"

One friend said, "no" because my husband and I don't go in saying,

"This is what you've got to do." We do try to go into things very open minded and wanting to listen. We try to learn from the people there. I get as much (if not more) out of the volunteer work and other stuff as I put into it, like we are always working on ourselves as much as we're working on helping other people. We know that we don't know. I think that in order to give help in the right way, you need to be able to accept help. So we do our best to listen and learn.

Brené Brown said something that always sticks out to me. She said, "I am not here to be right. I am here to get it right."

So if someone says, "This is not right," I don't feel bad. I feel like I'm learning something. It doesn't make me feel defensive or anything like that.

I know I was not conscious of what I was learning as a child. So for myself, and as a parent, I think I need to do the work to counter those messages

And we don't just volunteer either. In the beginning, this was partly because I didn't want my kids or anyone to think of us as White saviors, but now we just really enjoy spending time in Englewood. We go to Kusanya coffee shop because we love the vibe and the bagels there. My favorite spot is actually a construction site owned by our friend who is a builder in the neighborhood. He lets my kids climb around on stuff (safely of course!) and make pictures in the sawdust. So after we visit somewhere or we volunteer, we always try and find yummy treats somewhere. Last time, we went to Brown Sugar, a Black-owned bakery. And there's also these games and things that kids can play in, on the street in front of the bakery. So my kids are just having fun in Englewood, and I think it's really cool. Now they have memories and ideas of what Englewood is really about instead of just unconsciously absorbing or believing what's portrayed in the news (and/or shared by the people in our bubble).

I know I was not conscious of what I was learning as a child. So for myself, and as a parent, I think I need to do the work to counter those messages.

I think my parents, especially my dad, are scared. But he also respects the things that my husband Jeremy and I are doing and the beliefs that we have.

To me, it just feels like this is what we need to be doing. And I started to wonder, how come everyone is not doing this? So even though it feels funny, like I am trying to show off or something, I voice my opinions now. Sometimes I post my views on social media.

We just have so many issues now, not just race relations but things like climate change, poverty, and political chaos. I think the only way to move past those issues is through love. And you can't do that by staying apart from people.

My dad wants to learn more and do better, but he also has all the thoughts of White fragility and just that scared mentality of,

"I don't want anything bad to happen to you guys." But he is trying. And my parents never tell us not to do anything that we're doing. They always support us.

The first time I went to Englewood, I was scared mostly about being caught in gunfire, like somehow being an innocent bystander to somebody passing by and shooting. You just hear stories on the news about parents who don't let their kids go outside and play in Englewood so I'm like,

"Oh my God, I'm taking my kids here to do just that." That felt scary and very vulnerable for me. And this is super embarrassing to admit, but I called someone at I-Grow, the Englewood non-profit that runs Peace House, and I asked,

"Is it gonna be safe there?"

And as I was driving there, I remember being nervous about it. And I was like, I want to do this. I knew that it was what I wanted to do. I knew it was important to do it. But I was definitely worried about it. And I remember thinking,

"I'll be happy once we're driving away and we can be like, we have done this." Not "we did it, and it's over with," but "I'm glad that we safely did this."

But then I got to Peace House. And I felt a complete sense of peace. It was a beautiful day, and we were outside in the garden area. The kids were running around and playing with a couple of kids nearby. And I just remember feeling like,

"This is nice. I'm really, really glad we did this." And that sense of fear had gone away. I realized; this is just a street with kids hanging out. And now we go to Englewood frequently and I don't feel those same fears that I had before.

I grew up in Northbrook, a suburb on the North Shore of Chicago. It's a predominantly White upper-class neighborhood. I never thought about race or religion when I was growing up.

Many people were Jewish. Even more were White. Well, I had a couple of friends that were Korean, but race wasn't spoken about.

I don't even know that I had an idea about why there were no Black people in our neighborhood. That just wasn't something that crossed my mind.

I cannot think of a time where race was talked about or thought about or even, like, "Why are there no poor people here? Why is everybody just like us?" I feel like everyone acted the same. One of my only real cultural memories of that age was going to my good friend's house, who is Korean, and her mom made us this delicious rice dish. But that was really all I thought about at that time, regarding race.

And when I saw a Latino or a Black person in my childhood bubble, they were serving me or my family. I never even wondered what they liked to eat, or what their culture was like. And they were the busboys, not the waiters. They always had the jobs that were seen as less prestigious.

You know, I listened to rap music. I watched The Cosby Show. But I don't think it ever registered that the singers and the actors were Black. I never considered that there was anything different about their experiences. I don't know. I'm really trying to think. I'm sure I knew that the people on the screen were Black, but I just didn't think of it as anything different from this bubble that I've already got going on.

The fact that none of this was even in our consciousness is kind of the definition of White privilege; we just live this really nice happy existence where any problem is solvable.

I grew up feeling like I could accomplish anything I wanted. I could do anything I wanted to do, be anything I wanted to be. The world was my oyster. And not only that, but I didn't need to think about anybody else. Don't get me wrong. My family was giving. We donated stuff and helped in different ways, but I don't remember doing a lot of volunteering. But if we did, we didn't talk much about why some groups of people needed extra help.

Our country has so much White supremacy baked in that you're really not even aware of it when you're learning it. Like, I remember learning about the "happy slave" in school. Like, that's not even possible. Even if you were treated "well" by your master. And of course, there's no "good" master. I remember being like,

"Oh, phew, I'm from Chicago, that's the north. At least we didn't do *that*." And then I realized,

"Well, shit, we did a lot of shit. There was no official slavery, but we did a lot of things that were not right."

But then, that's not what I was taught. I was never taught the truth about Christopher Columbus. I think our whole curriculum was whitewashed. That's why I need to take the time now to re-learn our history so I can educate myself. I need to unlearn a lot of things I was taught.

I think it makes you a more complete person to be aware of the world. And I think it helps you understand who you are. Just being surrounded by the sameness, you're not ever really challenged to think about who you are, what you believe in, what's important to you. Because all you see is yourself, reflected back to you.

I didn't understand the importance of this really until I went to a Catholic college. That was eye-opening for me. Like, I didn't understand the personal value of my Jewish culture until my culture was in the minority. And seeing other people's cultures, other people's traditions, other people's ideas helped me see myself better, understand myself more, and eventually be more secure with myself.

I think seeing other people's cultures, other people's traditions, other people's ideas, opens you up to more understanding of yourself, which I think is the biggest gift in the world. You feel more secure when you understand yourself better. And I think that if we're not secure with ourselves, we can't go out there and be completely open and loving, and create the world that we want to be living in.

Maybe we evolved into being people who are afraid of differences. But now I think it's time for our next evolution. Like, if we are going to maintain humanity, people need to get out of that fear mindset and get into the love mindset.

And also, I think we need to understand that there's not a fixed amount of love. When we give love, we get more love in return. Love is not like a pizza. It's not like "when it's gone it's gone." Even if someone doesn't love us back, we get more love because we love ourselves more when we give love. So we all need to manifest love within ourselves if we want to manifest love outwardly in this world.

I mean, that's what this world needs. Kind of. To be burnt down and rebuilt.

JUMPING ROPE –
DOMINIC'S STORY

W HEN MY FAMILY MOVED FROM NEW ORLEANS TO LAS Vegas, our neighbors were Mexican, and they would babysit us. So, when I was 9 years old, that was the first time I ever had a tortilla. Which was just like,

"Oh wow, what is this magical food?"

And then hearing someone speak Spanish. Which was just like,

"Oh wow, what is this magical language?"

So just being in close proximity to my neighbors who spoke Spanish affected me. We helped each other out and took turns babysitting for each other. These personal interactions probably opened up other ways of viewing things for me.

Until the COVID shutdown, my then-husband and I ran an Airbnb in Little Village on the Southwest Side of Chicago. We have hosted about 500 guests in five years. Most of our guests were forgettable in the best way possible. In the sense that they enjoyed their stay, gave us positive feedback, and then went on their way. We didn't need to interact a whole lot.

But I remember one guest. Her profile picture was called "tourist." She was White, wearing a cardigan sweater. She texted us on the day she was due to arrive at our place.

I can't find the house.

Oh, we can help you. Tell us where you are.

Well, is your address on North Fairfield?

No, no, we are on South Fairfield.

Well, I tried. I can't find parking near you.

Oh really? There is plenty of parking right outside our house. Maybe you're at the wrong address?

No, I'm not. Thanks, but I really can't stay now. Can you please issue me a refund?

Well, I don't know. I don't think so.

Ok, well, I am actually in front of your house in my car.

Oh great! Then come on in.

No way. I've been in third world countries that don't look as bad as this.

About 10% of our guests were like this. And on our block, kids are always outside playing. People are out running errands or gardening or barbecuing or whatever while people roll by and shoot these accusations at us.

Wow, I just went right into the heaviest part of this. Sorry.

Anyway, back to the story. We tried to call the woman back. She wouldn't answer.

So then we modified our marketing, and we did a lot of hand-holding, pushing back against the Lyft driver's advice, things like that. We did this really weird dance to reassure our fearful guests, step by step. We learned that we had to be creative with our Airbnb listing after one too many experiences with people saying,

"Oh, this is a bad neighborhood. I don't feel comfortable at all."

So then we just started saying the unspoken thing out loud,

This is a multi-generational Black and Latinx neighborhood. Do your research to make sure you feel comfortable before booking. We were really explicit; by putting the truth right up there, we tried to get ahead of these misguided reactions.

So then we just started saying the unspoken thing out loud

But even after people booked, they still made comments. Like they'd say, beautiful house, but then they would look around and whisper to me,

"Hey, is it safe here?"

And then we had to ask,

"What makes you think that it wouldn't be safe here?" And then they were like,

"Oh well, I don't know. I'm just unfamiliar with the area."

Again, remember that kids and families and people were out and about while they're saying this stuff to us. And we live here too.

So we learned to say stuff to familiarize the neighborhood, like we named all of our neighbors. We told our guests that any foot traffic by our house was people who knew us, and/or our dogs. We said things like,

"Franco and Margie live behind us. All our neighbors know who we are. They know our dogs too." In fact, there are some people who don't know *our* names, but they know the names of our dogs. They'll walk by and greet the dogs by name and say things like,

"I like the new plant."

Everyone is friendly and always saying hi to each other.

We could spot the guests with hunched shoulders and lowered eyes juxtaposed against this super friendly neighborhood. I'd say this happened like 10% of the time.

So that was a frustrating experience, but it was even worse when people didn't say anything. Like sometimes we thought our guests had a great experience. Then when they posted a review, they were like

"Neighborhood seems a *little sketchy*, but nothing happened."

Then there were other people who antagonized the situation, like car service drivers who told people that our neighborhood was dangerous. I know this happened, because if I took a car service to my house, the drivers are almost always like,

"Do you live in THAT neighborhood? That is a really bad neighborhood, you better be careful." And I'm like,

"This is my home. We've lived here for seven years."

That leads to a whole separate conversation between me and the driver, where I defend our community in the hopes that maybe the driver will reconsider what he says next time he's in my neighborhood. I feel like drivers think they should give people advice about neighborhoods even when the driver doesn't know much about the community.

Guests sometimes said,

"Hey, we think everything is fine. But our driver mentioned that, you know, we should be careful around here."

Then I would say,

"For sure, but you need to be careful everywhere and anywhere in Chicago."

I don't think I'll ever live on the North Side. That's just not my vibe. I have friends all over, but I just love Pilsen on the lower West Side. I love Little Village where I live. And we have a really nice setup with our home.

I was comfortable moving here because most of my friends are people of color, mostly Mexican. My best friend is Mexican. We were roommates when we were young adults. I met him when we both worked at the Gap in Indiana. We just hit it off. He was living with his family at the time in Pilsen and I spent a lot of time with him and his family there.

So, I guess you can thank the Gap. Yeah. I met my best friend at the Gap and this friendship exposed me to the South and West Sides of Chicago.

I always tagged along to our group baseball games (even though I am not athletic). My friend circle is all diehard Southsiders who sort of gravitated me to this area.

So much of what's good in my life came from that brief time I worked at the Gap. The best friend I met was my first best friend. And my first straight best friend. He's still my best friend. I think everyone kind of cherishes those firsts. He literally brought me into his family. And I'm so grateful for my friendship with him and his family. I wouldn't have made the connections I made without him. I wouldn't have these great friends. My best relationships tie back to this kind of butterfly effect from a friendship. I'm just always really grateful that we met.

I guess a lot of my not going to the South Side much has to do with friendship. I have a really great friend that lives in Bronzeville now. He's lived there for a while, so now I'm wanting to know more. I'm going to the Bud Billiken parade in Bronzeville. I think that's the segue for me.

I don't listen when people tell me not to go somewhere. When we go on trips, I'm like, I'll go anywhere, just tell me where we should go. So if someone had said,

"This thing is happening here on the South Side," then I'd be like,

"Alright, I'll go there."

I'm not saying I'm more of a follower because that kind of sounds negative. But I'm more open to people making suggestions for me. It's easier somehow.

Growing up in New Orleans, you know it was super segregated. Lots and lots of racism. I'm so thankful that I had the opportunity to live in Vegas. But not because I like gambling or brand-new buildings. I don't even drink. That's not my vibe. But Las Vegas is just so diverse.

It seems like no one who lives in Las Vegas comes from Las Vegas. It's like a melting pot. I know that term is overused, but I went from an almost all-White New Orleans Catholic school with maybe three people of color in my classes to Las Vegas, where it was completely diverse. I went to school with all kinds of kids. I lived near all kinds of people – Mexican, Korean, Chinese, Black. So that shift probably helped me. Because I still see people I knew in New Orleans who are stuck with these very specific views. I feel so thankful that I didn't stay there. I had the opportunity to be around different types of people in school and in my neighborhood. That made a big difference.

Everybody in my family growing up went to Catholic school or private school. The vibe was like,

"You can't go to public schools because they're bad." And I could see that the students at public schools were primarily Black.

My dad says, "I judge everyone individually." My mom doesn't really talk about race.

My parents never really judged me or my partners because of race or gender or sexual orientation. I'm gay. I married a man who

is Mexican and White. And my sister-in-law is biracial. One of my brothers is dating a biracial Asian woman.

My parents support us in choosing the people we love and the friends we make. So the problem isn't micro, it's not what we do, who we hang with, that's never really an issue. The problem is mostly macro, predominantly because my parents grew up in White neighborhoods that experienced White flight in New Orleans. So they have a different view of the big picture.

I had a different experience. I made friends on a micro level, then I projected that experience onto a macro level. I want to know more about whole communities for the same reason I wanted to know more about tortillas. Just being like, oh, wow this is magical. I didn't realize this was a thing. How do I learn more about it?

> I want to know more about whole communities for the same reason I wanted to know more about tortillas. Just being like, oh, wow this is magical. I didn't realize this was a thing. How do I learn more about it?

If you spend all your time around only like-minded people, your curiosity is less likely to be sparked about something you don't know. You just bounce the same ideas and viewpoints off of one another.

But when you're around different people, you're like, "Oh, this is interesting. Where are they from? What can I learn from them?"

Relationships humanize people who you don't know. I feel like it's really bad to say, but it's harder for someone to be emotionally connected to something like segregation when they get their images of a group through media or friends who talk negatively about other races. They don't know anyone personally who has been affected by segregation, or even someone who knows someone who's been hurt by segregation. I feel like it's easier for people to say,

"Oh, well, I have the right viewpoint about Mexican people, even though I don't know anyone that's Mexican."

I listen to podcasts that give me a sense of connection to all different types of people rather than podcasts from people who have the same experiences as my group. If I was to give advice to my White friends, I would say,

Seek diverse friendships. If that is too challenging right now, seek diverse content that humanizes people from different groups. This might be easier because you can listen, but you can't respond.

So if you listen to podcasts of Black people and people of color, you can put a voice with a name. If there's a video, then you can put a name with a face too.

I also tried to nudge people with our business. I'd post about the racist Airbnb experiences on Instagram. So people see what happens. I'm like, just be mindful whenever you go. Remember, you're literally going into someone else's neighborhood. Don't be rude and ask questions like THIS.

We also provided books about the South Side, and books by Ta-Nehisi Coates and other Black authors in our Airbnb library too. If someone wanted to pinch a book during their stay, these anti-racist resources were right there, like a subliminal nudge for our guests.

As an Airbnb host, you want your guests to have a good experience. You want to provide everything you can to make sure that happens. And then when you have to also point out someone's racist ways, it just gets a little heavy for us. And so we ask ourselves,

"How far can we go with this while someone is on vacation, staying in our home?" So it's definitely this weird dance of like,

We didn't want to get a bad review. But we needed to say something. It's just different when you're forced to have frequent conversations about racism with people you barely know, who are paying you for service. So the dance was a little like jumping rope, trying to step lightly and land in the best place to say something.

My then-husband was slightly better at this than me. If he was the one home when guests arrived, he was a little better at strategically putting someone in their place without offending them. It's a weird dance for sure.

REFLECTIONS ON
FROM HURT TO HEALING

Segregation doesn't just harm the people who live in disinvested neighborhoods. We all lose out because we miss the chance to meet each other. Many of our stories focus on the damage done to people from the neighborhoods that many other people are told to avoid. Directly. Not indirectly through the disinvestment or avoidance of neighborhoods where Black and Brown people lived. But directly because people found out where they were from and made assumptions about them based on it (like the studies showing that employers sometimes discriminate based on an applicant's zip code). But our stories show that the hurt goes beyond this. The stories humanize the patterns and structures that sociologists have been studying for decades and humanize the impact of these stereotypes, not just on the structures but on the people living in them.

A person needs to do more than visit a Black urban neighborhood or meet a resident though, because personal connections only make a difference if we are willing to acknowledge and examine our defaults. To solve the problem of segregation, we need to go from being outsiders and tourists (who aren't all that interested in the daily lived experiences of neighborhood residents) to being personally engaged visitors who care about the residents. The stories in this section also show us how we can become curious

263

about who we might meet and what we might learn. Essentially, curiosity enables unlearning the hidden views that help create segregation. And we see that segregation costs all of us so much.

We have all probably heard about the perils of believing stereotypes about people. But we've probably thought less about the stereotypes we have about places.[12] In this section, we go one step further and consider how our stereotypes about places can cycle back and impact what we think about the people who live there. So on top of all the structural disadvantages that come from living in an under-resourced neighborhood, people from Don't Go neighborhoods have to navigate interactions that get shaped by where they are from. The looks. The pity. The assumptions of less-than-ness. As Leslie puts it, "people are just less curious about me." Roberto's story shows us that curiosity – done right – may provide the antidote to the entire cycle. A solution to place-ism.

Tiana's story shows how tiring it is to both be judged as an exception to some stupid rule based on where she's from, and the need to constantly defend where she is proud to be from. Tiana is a resilient defender. Her fatigue is more than understandable (and not atypical). Being: a woman in a male-dominated profession + Black in a predominantly White workplace + a resident of Englewood = battling discrimination and harmful assumptions about you and your life every single day. For those of you who are NOT from places others are told not to go, ask yourself what it would be like to do all that you do, and be all that you are, and on top of that have to defend yourself, your loved ones, and your community from near constant misguided assumptions. Tiring, right?

As for Danica, from the Fear section, her fatigue comes from having to convince people of the diversity of experiences within any given under-resourced neighborhood; and the toll of being the Black student in a class with mostly White students and having to be the educator and naming the elephant in the room (race and segregation) when professors and administrators warn (White) students (social workers, no less) about places to not go. Despite the irony that these White students are safer there than the Black students. Danica's story is also memorable for the raw honesty and humor shared by Tonika and Danica as they brainstormed clap backs to the ridiculous question they both get asked: Have you ever seen someone get shot?

The hurt of these perceptions is both direct and indirect. Directly, as in Eva's reflections (in the Messengers section), when she talks about how the service social workers provide is likely impacted by a desire for (mostly White) social workers to "get in and get out" when they are in a Don't Go neighborhood. And the job applicant who doesn't get the interview because they come from a "bad" neighborhood. And the people in need of services of all kinds (piano tuning to social work to taxi rides and plumbing) who can't get them because the providers "Won't Go."[13]

Zachary, Leslie, Tiana, Danica. They all show the hurt of these stereotypes – not just of people, but the places they live in: we all know you're not supposed to stereotype people; but as these stories reinforce, stereotypes of neighborhood go unchecked all the time.[14]

Or Kristine's story, full of exaggerated shortcuts (Mad Max and the Thunderdome anybody?) who then reflects on the equally ridiculous implications of these exaggerations that she was privy to through her job: three-quarters of the city should not have to apologize to a middle-aged White lady Lyft driver for where they live. But Kristine's move toward healing is based on the curiosity that has driven her to change her default on what she thinks about the South and West Sides. Which brings us to Roberto.

Roberto is an outsider with a "passport." He both has questions because he doesn't know the unwritten rules about race; and he doesn't understand the most important unwritten rule: we're not supposed to talk about it. His job and his natural curiosity mean that he is constantly told "Don't Go," so he's given this a lot of thought – both about the damage done by the Don't Go narrative, and the antidote to it: curiosity.

Amy is a great example of someone asking questions and indulging her curiosity in unexpected ways (Black Twitter is her best friend for learning about race) to unlearn the defaults – like her realization about the danger her White skin poses to a Black man she passes on the street and her attempts to disrupt the default.

Dominic (like many others, and like social scientists show repeatedly[15]) moved from hurt to healing because of inter-racial contact – some of which happened in the workplace. But also because when his parents White-flighted away from New Orleans' Black–White segregation, they did not land where many such White flighters land: a White neighborhood.[16] Rather, they landed in a diverse neighborhood in Las Vegas. He credits these experiences as planting the seeds of openness and setting him on a path to his most fulfilling relationships. Something segregation's forces are intent on denying many of us.

Jenny S.'s story focuses on the role of love in moving from hurt to healing. Her story has elements of every section in this book: the fear of taking her children to Englewood, the messengers (teachers and textbooks), and the shortcuts that she contends with when friends learn of her trips where she is not supposed to go. The personal experience of being there, and viewing it not as a volunteer experience, but as a neighborhood where her children can play and get bagels. That's where the healing began.

Leslie

It was difficult to decide what to ask Leslie after she shared her story of the hurt she felt. It's hard to think of any other interview in this project which expressed to this extent how segregation hurts us. We'd been talking mostly to people who have been told

"Don't Go" to the South Side. And they'd been explaining to us how they decided to explore the neighborhoods on their own or how they found out that the stereotypes weren't true. Leslie's story is part of the same issue, but from a different perspective. It was really touching and powerful to us.

When I (Maria) started studying segregation from the perspective of perceptions of communities, I was focused on how these perceptions impact people's housing decisions and our economic and housing policies.[17] But Leslie's story asks us to think more deeply about how people feel when they're cast as the embodiment of that misperceived community, treatment which is just wrong. People should be able to talk about their childhood and where they lived. Because place does matter, place does shape us in some ways. But place shouldn't shape what people think of you, what they assume about your abilities and your experiences and your life and your worth. It just makes us mad. And sad. We remember we both had tears in our eyes at the end of that interview.

But there was one thing that brought about a chuckle in Leslie's story: when saying that a lot of the (White) students at her university were students from St. Louis, from how she talked about them, they were acting like they never heard of segregation. But St. Louis is one of the most segregated cities in the country, just like Chicago. And what's interesting is that most of the times White people don't think of themselves as being segregated. They think, "oh, Black people and Latino people are segregated."

But when you ask White people if they live in a suburb or a part of Chicago where they only see White people, they're like, "wait what? Just because I only see White people? That means I'm segregated? Segregated from who?" Many White people are implicitly thinking "Black person growing up in an all-Black neighborhood" is what we mean by segregation. Well, if you grew up in a suburb with no Black people, you lived in a segregated neighborhood too.

We need to all realize, "No, we are all segregated. From each other. And it's not my fault or your fault. You were just born where you were born, like me, or you just decided to live where you live. You didn't think about it."

That's what we're talking about. That's the whole thing we are trying to change.

Section 5
Taking a Step to Take One More

Big systemic issues – and segregation is one of them – can feel overwhelming for individuals to tackle. And they are. But this doesn't mean that individuals don't matter. In fact, individual actions and personal relationships plant the seeds for the big solutions: collective action, policies, laws, and structural changes. One person can make a difference. As Jeff said, "I don't have to make it to the top of Mt. Everest. I just have to take the next step."

Luckily, the everyday people in this book have figured out many ways to disrupt segregation. Here, we'll review the ideas that enabled our storytellers to break through the barriers to change, the reasons why they thought it was so important, and the ways they navigated the journey to changing their defaults. We've divided these tips into three sections: Talking, Feeling, and Acting.

TALKING

A S WE EXPLAINED IN OUR INTRODUCTION TO THIS PROJECT, WE were worried about the impact of being together in the interviews. Would White people talk to a Black artist from Englewood about being told not to go to her neighborhood? And would Black people be willing to talk to a White sociologist about the hurt that (mostly White) people perpetuated? And if they were willing to be honest, would we all at one time or another be

Uncomfortable?

Embarrassed?

Awkward?

Apologetic?

Turns out that the answer to all four of these questions is a resounding yes.

But it also turned out that the presence of both of us together, who talked to each other and to the storytellers during the interviews, was reassuring. There were moments in the conversations where Tonika would translate something for Maria that she didn't understand – and vice versa. Would the stories have unfolded differently if Maria interviewed the White people and Tonika interviewed the Black people? We'll never know. But we do know that these stories are powerful and true. Something magical happened for sure.

We learned that it's hard to talk about this issue of systemic messaging and racism for many reasons.

Telling the truth about personal Don't Go experiences might

make people uncomfortable,

take a toll on everyone, including the people who have already been hurt by this messaging,

make people worry about what other people might think,

feel weird and confusing.

It's also hard to go against the idea that we should never talk about this. Most of us don't know how. What if we say the wrong thing?

To help you get past some of these barriers, here are some ideas about how to start talking about "Don't Go" in particular, and race in general.

When to Shut Up and When to Start Talking

→ Jeff reminds us that people (mostly White people) need to "shut up and listen to the voices you haven't heard before and are often shut down."

→ Tonika's strategy is to, "Shut up so others can listen to what they themselves just said, and let them process it and realize 'Oh, right. That was a really racist thing to say'."

→ Kristine's learned that knee-jerk reactions to her mother are not helpful at all. In fact, stopping and really listening to her mom before responding turned out to be far more effective than telling her mom she was wrong or dismissing her outright.

→ But taken too far, silence is dangerous: because silence in the face of blatant or even subtle messages about race and place is passively contributing to the problem.

→ Don't let embarrassment stop you. Accept the fact that the "right" way to talk about this can be elusive and sometimes you have to be willing to stumble through to figure it out. That happened more than once in our conversations.

It's helpful to know what to say and what not to say:

→ Don't call people naïve when they tell you that they went where they were told not to go. If someone calls you naïve, remember that courageous is another word for standing up to racist messaging no matter where it's coming from. And there's nothing wrong with being naïve – all it means is that you don't know something yet. And you're willing to admit that rather than follow racist advice.

→ Don't lead a conversation with an accusation. Instead of accusing someone of being just plain wrong about a neighborhood, take a breath, remind them that they are talking about people, and explain what's wrong with the message.

→ Don't just repeat what you hear. Ask yourself what you actually know about a place before you say anything.

→ If you have a friend who works in a place or lives in a place or wants to visit a place you've been told not to go, stop asking them if they feel safe. And just in case you missed it, don't ever ask a South or a West Side resident if they've witnessed a shooting!

→ Trust your lived experience. Going where you were told not to go and having nothing bad happen is more common than what you've been told by the media or heard from someone who heard it from someone else.

→ Recognize codewords and racist dog whistles. Numbers and statistics are codewords that need to be contextualized. Learn the specifics, the history, the explanation, and the parameters of the Don't Go messages you hear.

→ The question that might inspire someone to change doesn't have to be complicated. Maybe something as easy as: Is this *really* how we want to live? Or, Why do we make it so hard?

One of the goals of all this necessary talk is to help (White people especially) walk from sympathy to empathy. Even kind, charitable people describe the South and West Side neighborhoods with words like downtrodden. Unpacking this adjective can reveal the difference between sympathy and empathy.

We feel sorry that a place is downtrodden. But empathy is something else. In the Folded Map project, a Black woman named Nanette from the South Side said that she felt like her Map Twins, Wade (White) and Jennifer (Asian) from the North Side, *heard* her. Nanette said she felt *understood*. And Wade and Jennifer described being upset at the systemic forces that had put their friend Nanette in a precarious situation. Wade and Jennifer are expressing empathy, which enables a broader, more inclusive point of view. We see each other as peers, equals who have either been subjected to barriers or been gifted with advantages. We don't feel envious of or sorry *for* anyone. We feel personally involved in what is happening, almost as if it was happening to us. And we understand that it IS happening to us, in that we are disconnected from potential friends and new experiences. We are happy to see opportunities given to our friends and we are upset when our friends experience unfair disadvantages.

When people recognize the problems out there, but don't see people as peers, the feelings are of sympathy and guilt. White people get jammed up after presentations by Tonika. Because here they are, feeling sorry for this brilliant woman who has accomplished so much. It doesn't make sense. Then people also dive into the idea of exceptionalism. If this woman from Englewood managed to succeed, it must have been a long hard slog to get there. Both of these views – sympathy and oversized admiration – stop us from connecting. We only see the part we feel sorry for, or the part we admire for overcoming so many challenges. We don't see the full breadth of the human being in front of us.

Sympathy is a good first step, though. Then people can walk with us over to empathy.

FEELING

ONE OF THE GOALS OF TALKING IS THAT IT ADDRESSES THE feelings. During our conversation with Eva, who wrestled a great deal with how she navigated having people instill fear in her, Tonika was moved to assure her,

This fear you describe is a real part of the problem. If we're constantly instilling fear, how do people overcome that? And then you tell us how you actually overcame that fear. That's so important. Because you have to have this kind of conversation with your family. With your friends. I never even considered White people having to do that. If you are empathetic and trying to not be racist, you have to respond to people's reactions. And I just find your truth quite beautiful actually. I mean, I literally didn't go away to college because my mom approved my fear.

I think if people really understand what fear does and how one has to overcome it, they might understand. Like, you can't overcome it by just saying, "Oh, I have a friend that's Black." No, it's talking about exactly what you're sharing with us. So I just had to tell you, thank you. I really do appreciate your honesty, because it's not a lot of people want to have this conversation in this way. You know, the emotional part of it.

In other words, there are a lot of feelings wrapped up in the transmission – both giving and receiving – of Don't Go messages. Of those who live in the places people are told "Don't Go" as well as those who are told not to go.

→ Jenny feels scummy referring to the Don't Go neighborhood she worked in as "bad" when it had only ever been good to her.

→ Leslie is frustrated because people are not as curious about her when they find out where she's from.

→ Jenny S. is embarrassed when other White people see her as some kind of a hero for going to a Black neighborhood – and she's worried about acting like a "White savior."

→ Tiana is tired of having to defend her neighborhood.

→ Roberto and Sara were ashamed to ask someone if the Don't Go warnings were true.

→ Danica is annoyed at always being viewed as an exception because of where she's from.

During our conversation, Jerry offers a distinctly sociological analysis (not surprising, he is a sociologist after all) of the connection between feelings (the micro) and the systems that perpetuate segregation (the macro):

"This is the problem with racism. It's not about individual attitudes. The nature of this system makes it so that when a White person gets on a bus with all Black people, they're gonna feel something. They're probably not gonna feel nothing. It will feel different than getting on a bus with all White people. But if we're going to strive towards a world of not only dismantling racism on a larger level, but also just the interpersonal stuff, you have to walk through this and be willing to expose yourself to feelings about yourself that you might not be comfortable with."

And our book is full of people of all races who were willing to walk through this, and all the feelings of embarrassment, fatigue, frustration, confusion, talk to us, and tell us about the actions they took. And we have to get past the embarrassment and all the other feelings, or this cycle is never going to end.

ACTING

To kick this section off, we want to share one action that happened – in real time – during our conversation with Adrianne.

Adrianne received the "Don't Go" message early and often from her family – her grandmother in particular, who lived on the South Side. They were worried about her safety. But she also had a lot of fear once she decided to start pushing back against the racism she was witnessing. She worried about coming across wrong – for example, by publicly announcing she was looking for Black and Brown artists to promote at her store. It felt wrong given that she was supposed to be color blind. And she admitted she wasn't sure Black artists would make sense (or be interested) in her "bubbly and whimsical" store.

And, she said, she just didn't know any Black artists.

The power of breaking the barrier of segregated social networks and of personal connection leaped out across the Zoom screen when Tonika said "Well, you know me; and I know three," and shared the Instagram handles of three artists with Adrianne. And one thing led to another and Adrianne ended up featuring these artists in her store on a permanent basis, and being invited to birthday parties of her new friends' friends.

Not only did Adrianne go where she was told not to go, but she also found a way, through her business, to break more barriers. She took some steps, guided by imagination, to disrupt segregation. And it was transformative.

And she's not alone:

→ Jerry put his money where his mouth is – realizing that for all the books he was reading as a sociology graduate student, he needed to experience the city and Go. As Tonika says, "stop reading reports about Chicago's segregation and other problems as if they are about another city. Realize that it's us and our decisions that keep this cycle going."

→ Joey inspired us all with his willingness to challenge his social networks (touching people that books and experts cannot); slowly convincing them that the media's portrayal of Don't Go neighborhoods was incorrect.

→ Zachary and Jenny and Eva and many, many, others honed an equally "canned" response to the mindless repetition of "Don't Go" warnings. Ones that made people think, put things in perspective, and disrupted the narrative. Tiana nudged her new-to-town colleagues to consider *all* their options.

→ Aleya and Sara and Jamaine all pushed against the influence of "Don't Go" messaging when they were looking for a place to live; they asked extra questions, sought out different information sources, and landed somewhere they were told not to go.

→ Jerry and Aleya used social media to find the real story (and where the fun was) about the South and West Sides when they realized the traditional media were little help.

→ Tiana took her classmates to her home in Englewood – defying the campus security mandates to not go.

→ Dominic used his Airbnb experiences to educate people about the realities of racism and place-ism through social media posts and strategic placement of books about the South Side.

→ Leslie has crafted responses to make people think and wonder when they say disparaging and untrue things about the neighborhood she grew up in.

→ Amy follows Black Twitter to educate herself about racism in America (on top of all the books she reads and documentaries she watches).

→ Jamaine refuses to let CNN and Fox tell him about a place.

→ Danica calls into question the claims that her White classmates will be in danger on the South Side.

→ Jeff is trying to raise his child so that anti-racist ideas come to him as naturally as racism came to him. And he is working hard to shut up and listen.

→ Tiana invited her classmates to her home in Englewood for Thanksgiving – the classmates that were warned by school staff on their first day to never go there.

→ Kristine refused to avoid the South Side as a Lyft driver and learned how to adapt her behavior as a White woman when encountering Black men.

To break the bubbles in a way that doesn't require Black people to spend time educating White people all the time:

Listen to podcasts of and by Black people.

Post on social media your experiences observing and learning about racism and / or going where you are told not to go.

Follow Black Twitter so you can have all your awkward questions answered without burdening people of color.

Find the non-traditional (often social) media sources that provide information about events, restaurants, stores, and opportunities in Don't Go neighborhoods.

Follow new people to mess with your algorithms.

Finally, remember to always pay attention to the ending. To understand the impact of what you say to people about the neighborhoods you visit, take a look at what could have happened if our storytellers had listened to Don't Go messages.

I was the only White person on the bus.

It felt so uncomfortable. It was so scary.

I never went on that bus again.

The presenter at my college orientation told everyone it was not safe to go to this one neighborhood.

That was where I lived.

I never told anyone where I lived.

When I came back from a job and told my coworkers where I had been, they all flipped out.

You made it back alive? You should NEVER go there again. Do you have a death wish?

I never went back there again.

I was so excited about my first job after graduation. It was in Englewood.

Everyone was telling me how crazy I was for working there.

I quit the next week.

At my college orientation I was so excited about being in college. Then people found out where I had grown up.

Everyone was telling me how dangerous my neighborhood was, and they looked at me like I was "hood."

I never went back.

These are the versions that we DIDN'T hear. Because our storytellers realized that the messages that people mindlessly repeat are harmful. They became agents of positive change.

They rejected the accusation that they were naïve and proudly claimed their own realities.

They proudly defended their neighborhoods.

They shut up and listened.

Tonika: I learned from the people we interviewed that they feel vulnerable when they first stop following the advice, "Don't Go." And I think being vulnerable connects people in a very powerful way. Instead of thinking of it as a social justice project, maybe think about it as just a personal thing. You might meet your new best friend or find your favorite restaurant on the South Side. I mean, that's what segregation makes us miss – new, fun, interesting people, places, and experiences. This is what I want people to know – I don't want to miss meeting you and I don't want you to miss meeting me just because of where we live. Just because someone told you not to go to my neighborhood.

NOTES

1 Data sources for racial composition of Chicago are as follows: the 2010 US Census Centers of Population (for the locations of the population weighted centroids for Census Tracts); and the 2017–2021 American Community Survey 5-year estimates (for the race/ethnicity estimates).

2 John R. Logan and Brian J. Stults. 2021. "The Persistence of Segregation in the Metropolis: New Findings from the 2020 Census." Diversity and Disparities Project. Brown University. Available at https://s4.ad.brown.edu/Projects/Diversity

3 See, for instance, George Galster and Patrick Sharkey. 2017. "Spatial Foundations of Inequality: A Conceptual Model and Empirical Overview," *Journal of the Social Sciences*, Vol. 3, No. 2, pp. 1–33.

4 Data sources used in these figures are:

    (1) Demographic, economic, education, and housing data are from: https://robparal.com/chicago-data/

    (2) Vacant housing unit data are from: https://www.cmap.illinois.gov/documents/10180/126764/Lake+View.pdf (Lakeview) and https://www.cmap.illinois.gov/documents/10180/126764/Englewood.pdf (Englewood)

    (3) Banks and restaurants data: https://experience.arcgis.com/experience/4041a85bcd0a4bc7a546aad03692c9f9/page/2)-EXPLORE-neighborhoods/

    (4) Grocery store (excluding corner stores) data are from the City

of Chicago Data Portal: https://data.cityofchicago.org/Health-Human-Services/Grocery-Store-Status-Map/rish-pa6g

5   If you want to read more about the causes of segregation, here's a reading list to get you started: James H. Carr and Nandinee K. Kutty (eds). 2008. *Segregation: The Rising Costs for America*. Routledge. Sheryll Cashin. 2022. *White Space, Black Hood: Opportunity Hoarding and Segregation in the Age of Inequality*. Penguin. Sheryll Cashin. 2005. *Failures of Integration: How Race and Class Are Undermining the American Dream*. PublicAffairs. Elizabeth Korver-Glenn. 2021. *Race Brokers: Housing Markets and Segregation in 21st-Century Urban America*. Oxford University Press. Maria Krysan and Kyle Crowder. 2017. *Cycle of Segregation: Social Processes and Residential Stratification*. Russell Sage Foundation. Douglas S. Massey and Nancy A. Denton. 1998. *American Apartheid: Segregation and the Making of the Underclass*. Harvard University Press. Andre M. Perry. 2020. *Know Your Price: Valuing Black Lives and Property in America's Black Cities*. Brookings Institution Press. Richard Rothstein. 2018. *The Color of Law: A Forgotten History of How Our Government Segregated America*. W.W. Norton. Keeanga-Yamahtta Taylor. 2021. *Race for Profit: How Banks and the Real Estate Industry Undermined Black Homeownership*. University of North Carolina Press.

6   bell hooks. 2018. *All About Love: New Visions*. William Morrow Paperbacks.

7   This idea, and how it contributes to residential segregation, is laid out in Maria's 2017 book with Kyle Crowder, *Cycle of Segregation: Social Processes and Residential Stratification*. Russell Sage Foundation.

8   Natalie Y. Moore. 2016. *The South Side: A Portrait of Chicago and American Segregation*. Macmillan.

9   Check out these books if you want to read more:
Gerd Gigerenzer, Peter M. Todd, and ABC Research Group. 2000. *Simple Heuristics that Make Us Smart*. Oxford University Press.
Richard H. Thaler and Cass R. Sunstein. 2021. *Nudge: The Final Edition*. Penguin.

10 Coined by Thaler and Sunstein (see note above).

11 James Baldwin. 1962. "Letter from a Region in My Mind," *The New*

Yorker, November 17. Available at https://www.newyorker.com/magazine/1962/11/17/letter-from-a-region-in-my-mind

12 Courtney M. Bonam, Hilary B. Bergsieker, and Jennifer Eberhardt. 2016. "Polluting Black Space," *Journal of Experimental Psychology: General*, Vol. 145, No. 11, pp. 1561–82.

13 On the impacts of this kind of employment discrimination and retail redlining, see, for example:

Marianne Bertrand and Sendhil Mullainathan. 2004. "Are Emily and Greg More Employable Than Lakish and Jamal? A Field Experiment on Labor Market Discrimination," *The American Economic Review*, Vol. 94, No. 4, pp. 991–1013.

Denver D'Rozario and Jerome D. Williams. 2005. "Retail Redlining: Definition, Theory, Typology, and Measurement," *Journal of Macromarketing*, Vol. 25, No. 2, pp. 175–86.

14 A good place to read up on this is, again, Courtney M. Bonam, Hilary B. Bergsieker, and Jennifer Eberhardt. 2016. "Polluting Black Space," *Journal of Experimental Psychology: General*, Vol. 145, No. 11, pp. 1561–82.

15 Examples include: Cynthia Estlund. 2003. *Working Together: How Workplace Bonds Strengthen a Diverse Democracy*. Oxford University Press. Thomas F. Pettigrew and Linda R. Tropp. 2006. "A Meta-Analytic Test of Intergroup Contact Theory," *Journal of Personality and Social Psychology*, Vol. 90, No. 5, pp. 751–83.

16 Lincoln Quillian. 2002. "Why is Black-White Residential Segregation So Persistent?: Evidence on Three Theories from Migration Data," *Social Science Research*, Vol. 31, pp. 197–229.

17 Maria Krysan and Michael D.M. Bader. 2007. "Perceiving the Metropolis: Seeing the City through a Prism of Race," *Social Forces*, Vol. 86, No. 2, pp. 699–733. Michael D.M. Bader and Maria Krysan. 2015. "Community Attraction and Avoidance in Chicago: What's Race Got to Do with It?" *Annals of the American Academy of Political and Social Science*, Vol. 660, No. 1, pp. 261–81.

IMAGE CREDITS